To

March 14, 2019

Predictors of Victory and Injury in Mixed Martial Arts Combat

A Scientific Study of Professional Fight Records

Hooman Estelami, Ph.D.
Fordham University

Bahar Books

**In memory of the ten fighters
who have lost their lives in
mixed martial arts competition:**

Booto Guylain (Congo, 2014)
Felix Pablo Elochukwu (Canada, 2013)
Tyrone Mimms (United States, 2012)
Mike Mittelmeier (Bolivia, 2012)
Dustin Jenson (United States, 2012)
Michael Kirkham (United States, 2010)
Sam Vasquez (United States, 2007)
Lee (Korea, 2005)
Douglas Dedge (United States, 1998)
Alfredo Castro Herrera (Mexico, 1981)

TABLE OF CONTENTS

CHAPTER 1: INTRODUCTION   1

CHAPTER 2: DATA AND METHODOLOGY   9

    Sources of Data   10
    Methodology for Data Analysis   15

**CHAPTER 3: PATTERNS OF VICTORY IN MIXED
MARTIAL ARTS COMBAT**   21

    Does Age Affect a Fighter's Ability to Win?   24
    Does Age Affect How a Fighter Wins?   28
    Does Being Younger Affect One's
    Chances of Winning?   31
    Does Weight Class Affect How One Wins?   33

**CHAPTER 4: PATTERNS OF INJURY IN MIXED
MARTIAL ARTS COMBAT**   37

    How Many Injuries Do Fighters Typically
    Experience?   38
    What Types of Injuries Do
    Fighters Experience?   40
    Have Injury Rates Changed Over Time?   41
    Does Age Affect the Number of Injuries
    Experienced During a Fight?   43
    Does the Difference Between
    Combatants' Ages Affect Injury Rates?   44
    Does Weight Class Affect Injury Rates?   45

**CHAPTER 5: EFFECTS OF THE FIGHT CONTEXT
ON FIGHT OUTCOMES**   49

Are Title Fights More Likely to Result in
Non-Decision Conclusions?   51
Does the Length of the Fight Influence
the Outcome?   52
Does the Position on the Card Influence
How a Fight Ends?   54
Have Fight Outcomes Evolved
Over the Years?   56
Are Fighters from Certain Countries
Better than Others?   57
Is there a Hometown Advantage?   59

CHAPTER 6: THE FIGHTER VERSATILITY INDEX   61

Data Source   62
Computing Win and Loss Ratios   63
What are Typical Win and Loss Ratios?   67
How do Win Ratios Change Over Time?   69
Can Fighter Versatility Be Quantified?   70
What are Typical Versatility
Levels for Fighters?   73
Does a Loss Lead to a
Win in the Next Fight?   74
Do Early Signs of Fighter Success Exist?   76
Does Experience Give
a Fighter an Advantage?   77
What Other Performance
Measures Exist?   79

**CHAPTER 7: THE EFFECTS OF FIGHTER HEIGHT
AND REACH**   81

What are Typical Fighter Frame Sizes?   84
Do Frame Size Differences
Influence Win Rates   85
How Do Advantages in Reach and Height
Influence the Method of Winning?   88
Does the Fighter's Stance
Influence Fight Outcomes?   89

CHAPTER 8: PREDICTING FIGHT OUTCOMES   93

What Variables Can Be
Used for Prediction?   95
What Statistical Method Can Be
Used for Predicting Fight Outcomes?   97
Can Fight Outcomes Be Predicted?   99
Are the Predictions Useful?   101

CHAPTER 9: FIGHT RITUALS   105

What Are the Most Common Pre-fight
Acknowledgements Inside the Cage?   108
Does the Fighters' Lack of Mutual
Acknowledgement Lead to Violent Endings? 109
Does Taking the Center of the Cage in
the Opening Round Matter?   111
Do Fighters Typically Carry Over
Lack of Mutual Acknowledgment
to the End of the Fight?   112
How Frequently Do Winners Exhibit Signs
of Spirituality at the End of the Fight?   114

**CHAPTER 10: IMPLICATIONS FOR THE FUTURE
OF MIXED MARTIAL ARTS**   115

Implications for Fight Promoters
and Regulators   116
Implications for Medical Care Providers   119
Implications for Trainers and Fighters   121
Concluding Thoughts   125

PREFACE

The explosive growth of mixed martial arts (MMA) over the past two decades is undeniable. By some estimates, MMA is the fastest growing spectator sport in the world. Although variations of MMA have been practiced for centuries in almost every corner of the world, its recent commercialization has changed its status to a mainstream sport with a following rivaling that of other popular sports. MMA events now attract millions of viewers through pay-per-view television, and thousands of spectators attend live fights across the globe. Every year, thousands of fighters face each other in professional bouts. Despite the mass-commercialization of the sport today, MMA has challenged long-held views, some dating back centuries, on what constitutes effective hand-to-hand combat.

With the explosive growth of the sport comes a huge amount of data. The nature of MMA competitions lends itself to the collection of data in specific categories, such as the physical characteristics of the fighters and the outcomes of the fights. The massive amount of accumulated data now enables us to apply statistical methods of analysis in order to predict the drivers of victory and defeat inside the cage with increased accuracy. We can now ask a wide range of questions about the specific conditions that facilitate combat success and find the answers to these questions by methodically analyzing the accumulated data. The vast amounts of collected data allow statistical science to be applied in order to validate the effectiveness of hand-to-hand combat methods in competitive settings, perhaps for the first time in human history.

My pursuit of this analysis was inspired by my own personal interest in various martial arts styles. Martial arts training challenges the practitioner beyond the limits of typical daily experiences and demands. The challenges are both physical and psychological. In almost every style of martial art, the practice demands from the practitioner emotional, mental and physical balance and refinement. Mixed martial arts takes individual development to a new level as it requires the practitioner to move beyond compliance with a single style in order to become fluidly skilled at a range of offensive and defensive techniques. By blending a range of styles, MMA represents the evolution of thousands of years of combat tradition into an effective and complex art.

Along with many others, I have remained interested in MMA because of its complex and multi-faceted nature while the field has continued to evolve over the past two decades. As a university professor who focuses upon the pursuit of empirical truths, I began to develop a scientific curiosity about the data that accumulated from MMA fights as the sport grew over the years. The analyses presented in this book include a compilation of research that has taken me several years to complete. Acknowledgments must be made to those who assisted with this work. First, I owe a great deal to my home institution, Fordham University, for all the support it has provided me during my research endeavors over the years. The academic culture at Fordham encourages intellectual curiosity and fosters scientific inquiry, even if the topic of research is as unique as that of this book. The support of the Father William E. Boyle Society at Fordham University was instrumental in facilitating this study.

Special thanks are also due to Frank Dehel, whose efforts were critical to the formation of data sets related to the first five chapters of this book. In addition, the help of Emi Hamo and Daniel Gaffey, who organized the data associated with chapters 6 to 8, is much appreciated. Sharon Mcclintic's methodical coding of fight rituals contributed to the analyses presented in chapter 9. The advice of Keith Keizer at the Nevada State Athletic Commission was essential in identifying the relevant data used in this book, and I am very appreciative of his support. I also want to thank Dean Bellantoni of the UFC Gym in Mamaroneck, NY for his exemplary professionalism in running this facility and for having given me access to it for nearly half a decade. I would also like to thank Molly Singleton-Coyne, who served as the editor for this book. Her input and feedback has helped a great deal in improving the quality of this work. Last, and certainly not least, I must thank my wife Nazanin. She has been a source of inspiration and support throughout this undertaking and encouraged me every step of the way. Had it not been for her support, this (and many other projects) would have probably never completed. She has been the most supportive spouse one could ever ask for.

It is important to acknowledge that this book focuses exclusively on men's MMA and does not include statistical analysis on data from women's MMA competitions. This is primarily due to the fact that the majority of MMA events held over the years include very few women's MMA bouts; therefore, there is currently a lack of sufficient data needed to conduct detailed statistical analysis on women's MMA. Analysis was performed solely on men's MMA because this was the context in which sufficient data exists; therefore, all fighters are referred to as masculine throughout the text of this book. However, as women's MMA grows in popularity and the related fight data records become more populated, the scope of such investigations can and should be expanded.

It is hoped that the information provided in these chapters will aid professionals in this field to better understand the sport, including its risks and its potential for development. Using the information provided in this work, athletes and trainers can better gauge opportunities and threats related to upcoming fights. Health care professionals whose duties include providing medical support to injured fighters may better understand resulting injuries and, therefore, provide more appropriate treatment because of the analyses presented in this book. For regulators and promoters of MMA events, it is hoped that the discussions presented in this book will inspire better methods of protection for athletes while maintaining the excitement and engagement that fans of the sport have enjoyed over the years. For the millions of passionate fans, it is hoped that a detailed picture of the complex dynamics of that which takes place inside the MMA cage will be provided by this book. Most importantly, I hope this book demonstrates the value of using scientific methods to develop irrefutable theories on combat effectiveness.

CHAPTER ONE
INTRODUCTION

It was November of 1993. In a packed stadium in Denver, Colorado, the top martial artists from around the world had gathered in what was to become a turning point in the history of combat sports. Named the Ultimate Fighting Championship (UFC), this was the first large-scale, high-profile mixed martial arts competition. It brought dozens of fighters from different fighting traditions together.

The intent was to determine the most effective combat style by holding a multistage tournament whereby practitioners of different martial arts styles would compete. The dominant opinion at the time, which prompted the organization of this event, was that strict adherence to traditional martial arts forms had unnecessarily limited the types of attacks fighters had been allowed to execute during a match. For example, a Karate practitioner was not allowed to grapple with his opponent, just as a Judo practitioner was not allowed to punch or kick his opponent. The relaxation of these rules would create a scenario more reflective of true hand-to-hand combat, which might prove some styles to be more effective than others. The lifting of combat restrictions prompted the fighters, promoters and the audience to focus on a single question on the night of the competition: *What happens when the rules are relaxed and the competitive combat scenario begins to resemble a true street fight?*

The November 1993 MMA event was not the first no holds barred contest of its type. There have been many similar tournaments, some taking place centuries ago[1]. However, the highly public forum of the first UFC event had a lasting effect on modern views of the effectiveness of various martial arts styles. The world of combat sports forever changed

---

[1] Clyde Gentry (2011). *No Holds Barred: The Complete History of Mixed Martial Arts in America.* Triumph Books.

that night. The traditional views that certain martial arts styles are more effective than others in combat settings were discredited. Audiences were baffled as Royce Gracie managed to repeatedly submit multiple opponents in consecutive bouts, demonstrating that classical views of combat, many embedded in hundreds of years of tradition, found little effectiveness inside the cage. Gracie was able to maneuver his opponents to the ground where most fighters were unfamiliar with ground fighting, and then apply submission techniques which would render his opponents unconscious or result in severe injuries to their joints. Needless to say, his opponents decided to tap out rather than to face these severe outcomes. Since then, the world of combat sports has continued to evolve. Styles such as Brazilian Jujitsu (BJJ) and Muay Thai have benefited many combatants in the cage over the past two decades. In addition, familiarity with hybrid forms of combat training including blends of boxing, Karate, Muay Thai, wrestling, and BJJ have become essential for fighters' success in mixed martial arts competitions. Since 1993, thousands of fighters have entered and exited the cage, half of whom have experienced victory, and the other half defeat.

The November 1993 competition revealed to the world how combat methods can evolve to become more effective, as well as how the relaxation of fighting rules can result in outcomes that differ significantly from those predicted by past fighting contexts. Since then, mixed martial arts has become one of the fastest growing spectator sports worldwide. While only a handful of states sanctioned mixed martial arts events in the sport's early stages, today many states in the U.S. sanction these events. The sport has also grown significantly on the international front, drawing fighters and spectators from around the globe.

From an academic perspective, the accumulation of large volumes of data from the thousands of fights that have taken place over the past two decades paves the path for scientific analysis of the conditions that facilitate successful outcomes for fighters inside the cage. The growing popularity of mixed martial arts has had an effect beyond increased viewership and public awareness of a new sport. As the sport grew over the years, the volume of fight data collected through sanctioning bodies has also grown. This data can be subjected to detailed scientific analysis, enabling us to study the conditions that facilitate victory in mixed martial arts combat.

Interestingly, the use of combat data to articulate conditions that facilitate combat success is anything but new. One of the most widely cited studies of combat strategy is the classical work of Carl von Clausewitz, which dates back nearly 200 years. As a general in the Prussian army, Clausewitz was fascinated by how success is achieved on the battlefield. In order to address this question, he methodically examined detailed records of battlefield engagements dating back to early recorded human history. In each case, he noted the conditions of the battlefield, the resources and capabilities of the combatants, and the outcomes of the battle. By doing so, he was able to formulate strategies that predict battlefield success. His work was eventually compiled as the classic book *On War*, and is now considered so fundamental to military science that it is required reading in most military academies around the world. It is in the same spirit of that work that the inquiry in this book takes place. The analyses provided in this book are inspired by detailed fight data from thousands of cage fights over a time period of two decades. The data are subjected to scientific analysis with the same purpose as that of Clausewitz two centuries ago: to uncover the drivers of victory in battle.

The observations in this book utilize established statistical methods and are aimed at the development of accurate theories about conditions that foster victory inside the cage. Individual observers of mixed martial arts combat may have personal theories as to what conditions increase the probability of victory. Often, these theories are central to conversations surrounding fights, as well as fight outcome speculations expressed in the media. However, for each of us, the theories that produce such predictions may be driven by one's own observations from the past. These observations are often gathered during the viewer's experience of past fights, commentators' discussions about the fights, reading up on the topic, or other sources. For example, one may speculate that taller fighters are more effective in striking, or that heavier fighters inflict greater physical damage to their opponents. Due to the constrained number of observations and the absence of systematic, statistical and scientific analysis, however, these theories may have limited accuracy. The accuracy of these theories can only be established through empirical research involving a large number of fights and cannot be validated reliably through individual ad hoc observations. The ability to develop and test theories using data is crucial to the development of foundational theories in any field. In mixed martial arts, the large volume of fight data accumulated over the years enables the researcher to conduct systematic testing of layman's theories on mixed martial arts competition outcomes, and to develop a rigorous conceptual framework for practitioners in the field.

The purpose of this book is to identify theories about success in mixed martial arts combat and to submit detailed fight data to scientific analysis in order to test the validity of these theories. Chapter 2 will include a discussion of the various data sources used in this book. In the chapter following that, we will examine the effects of fighters' age and weight on fight outcomes. Chapter 4 will focus on the physical injuries experienced by combatants and Chapter 5 will focus on the effect of the fight context on fight outcomes. Chapter 6 discusses measures used to quantify fighter capabilities based on a fighter's previous fight records and Chapter 7 will further examine the impact of a fighter's physical characteristics on the likelihood of winning fights. Chapter 8 will build upon this information by presenting a prediction model for predicting fight outcomes. Chapter 9 will discuss the role of pre-fight and post-fight rituals and their relationships with fight outcomes. The concluding chapter in this book will detail practical implications for fighters, trainers, medical care providers, promoters and regulators of mixed martial arts events.

CHAPTER TWO
DATA AND METHODOLOGY

The approach used in this book capitalizes on the power of large amounts of data to statistically test specific theories on mixed martial arts competition. As individual spectators the viewing of mixed martial arts tournaments may help us develop personal theories about fighting. Because the number of observations that a single individual can make is limited, however, the accuracy of any theory developed from such observations is also limited.

However, the more frequently one observes and analyzes conditions and outcomes of combat, the more complete one's understanding of fighting success may become. As the number of observations increases, and as the methods of analyzing these observations become more scientific, the theories for predicting combat success become more precise.

It is, therefore, critical to utilize established scientific methods when formulating foundational theories surrounding combat success. For this reason, the methods used in this book rely on the use of large-scale data captured through publically available fight records. The abundance of records on years of sanctioned mixed martial arts fights has made it possible to subject combat data to detailed statistical analysis, enabling us to test and validate theories of fighting with precision. The statistical methods used in this analysis are heavily relied upon in other fields of science such as sociology, psychology and biology, and have helped practitioners in these fields transform empirical observations into theories that are predictive of a range of phenomena within their respective domains of study.

Sources of Data

Chapters 3 to 5 focus on physical characteristics of fighters and fight contexts in terms of their effects on fight outcomes. The data for the analyses included in these three chapters were sourced from the Nevada State Athletic Commission post-fight reports. These reports are filed by the Commission following each MMA fight that takes place in the state of Nevada. Because of Nevada's long-held tradition of hosting combat sports events, the volume of fight records compiled by the Commission provides the wealth of information needed for the statistical analyses documented in these chapters. The analyses were performed on records documenting data from 1,178 mixed martial arts fights held in the state of Nevada between the years 2003 and 2010. For each fight, the Commission provided data on the physical attributes of the fighters, including each fighter's weight and age. In addition, data were recorded detailing the outcomes of each fight, including the numbers and categories of injuries, as well as the fight results (for example, knockout, technical knockout, submission, or decision). Additional information about each fight, such as the length of the fight, whether the fight was a title fight, the order of the fight in the tournament card, and other contextual variables, were also captured in the records. Exhibit 2.1 provides a summary of this data.

Exhibit 2.1: Data Fields in the
Nevada State Athletic Commission's MMA Fight Records

Fighter Characteristics:
- Fighter's date of birth
- Fighter's weight at time of weigh-in
- Fighter's home state/country

Fight Outcomes:
- Fight results (win/loss/draw/disqualification)
- How the fight ended (e.g., decision, TKO, etc.)
- Number of rounds to fight completion
- Length of fight completion
- Whether the fighter was disqualified or not
- Ringside physician's detailed injury report

Context of the Fight:
- Date of the fight
- Whether or not the fight is a title fight
- Order of the fight on the tournament card

Chapters 6 to 8 present models for predicting fight outcomes. In order to develop these models, professional fight records for hundred of fighters who had participated in fights between May 1996 and May 2013 were compiled. Official detailed fight records were analyzed for each professional MMA event in which these professional fighters competed. The records include data on the result (for example, win, loss, draw, etc) and the method by which the result was reached (for example, knockout, submission, etc.) as well as detailed information on the fighters' physical characteristics (for example, weight, height, reach, etc.) This data is openly accessible on the Internet from a variety of sources and can be studied in order to obtain details about a fighter's combat history. Exhibit 2.2 provides an outline of the data fields used in Chapters 6-8.

Exhibit 2.2: Data Fields Used For
Combat Outcome Prediction

Fighter Characteristics:
- Age
- Weight
- Height
- Reach
- Stance (orthodox vs. southpaw)

Fighter's Past Records (prior to the fight):
- Ratio of total wins over total fights
- Percentage of past fights won by decision
- Percentage of past fights won by KO or TKO
- Percentage of past fights won by submission
- Percentage of past fights lost by decision
- Percentage of past fights lost by KO or TKO
- Percentage of past fights lost by submission

Fight Outcome:
- Method of fight ending (TKO, KO, decision, etc.)
- Timing of fight ending (round and minutes)

Fight Context:
- Date of the fight
- Organization hosting the event
- Location where the event took place

Chapter 9 explores pre-fight and post-fight rituals exhibited by fighters. The data used in this chapter were obtained through extensive coding of video recordings of MMA tournaments. The tabulated data include the acknowledgements between combatants at the start of the fight (for example, whether or not they tap gloves), whether a fighter takes the center of the cage at the start of the first round, whether a winning fighter exhibits elements of spirituality upon achieving victory (for example, by pointing to the heavens) and if the fighters acknowledge each other when the official fight outcome is announced. Other measures such as each fighter's physical characteristics and the method by which victory was achieved are also analyzed, and the relationship between these measures and fight rituals is examined. Exhibit 2.3 provides a summary of this data.

Exhibit 2.3: Data Utilized to Examine Fighter Rituals

Fighter Characteristics:
- Age
- Weight
- Height
- Reach
- Country of birth

Pre-Fight Rituals:
- Does the fighter tap hands/fist with opponent?
- Does the fighter take the center of the cage at start of the fight?

Post-Fight Rituals:
- Does the fighter acknowledge opponent at the end of the fight?
- Does the winning fighter exhibit signs of spirituality at the end of the fight?

Fight Outcome:
- Method of victory (TKO, KO, decision, etc.)

Methodology for Data Analysis

The collected data are subjected to statistical analysis. The statistical methods used enable us to determine if relationships exist among the variables listed in the above tables, and if these relationships are strong enough to validate certain hypotheses. The purpose of this form of testing is to ensure that the observed results are not limited to the contexts in which the data were collected, meaning that the findings can generalize to other situations. This establishes patterns of relationships observed among specific variables that represent underlying phenomena. Using this approach we can empirically validate theories on combat effectiveness in competitive MMA settings.

The data analysis methods used in this book are heavily relied upon by scientists in various fields to test hypotheses and to develop theories that can accurately predict future outcomes. As some readers may be unfamiliar with them, a brief overview of these methods will be provided below. Interested readers are encouraged to further study these statistical techniques by consulting the appropriate statistical texts.[2] There are four basic types of

---

[2] A recommended resource is: J.F. Hair, W.C. Black, B.J. Babin, and R. E. Anderson (2010). *Multivariate Data Analysis*. Prentice Hall.

relationships that are examined frequently throughout this book:

(1) Relating two categorical variables: For example, we may be interested in knowing how the age category of a fighter relates to whether or not he wins or loses a fight. Both of these variables are categorical in nature, as they reflect the categorization of a fighter into a specific group (for example, a fighter in the 25-29 years old age range who has won his fight). To relate categorical variables, we report percentage figures associated with each category. For example, we may report that fighters in the 25-29 age category have a higher win probability than those in the 30-34 age category (for an example, see Exhibit 3.1 in the next chapter). To determine that the differences observed in percentage wins across the age categories are not a result of randomness in the data, and to ensure that the results would replicate in other situations (for example MMA fights in the future), a statistical test called Chi-square (pronounced "ki", not "chi") analysis is used. Two essential measures emerge from this test: the "p value" and the "Phi coefficient". The p value takes on a figure between 0 and 1. The threshold that is applicable to it is 0.05. When the p value is less than 0.05, we can conclude that a statistically significant relationship exists, and that the results observed establish a specific hypothesis or theory, such that most likely (specifically speaking

95% of the time) it will replicate in other fight contexts. A relaxed cut-off level for the p value is 0.1, which ensures that the results can be replicated 90% of the time (rather than the more strict level of 95% associated with a p value cutoff of 0.05). The second measure that emerges from Chi-square analysis is the Phi coefficient (denoted in the statistical outputs shown in this book as the Greek letter Φ). This measure takes on a value between -1 and 1 and its absolute value is reflective of the strength of the relationship. The higher the absolute value of Φ, the greater the strength of the relationship. For example, if one analysis yields a Φ value of 0.2 while another analysis using the same types of variables produces a Φ value of -0.4, the second analysis shows a stronger relationship (since the absolute value of -0.4 is 0.4 which is greater than 0.2) and can be more predictive of the outcome of events.

(2) Relating a categorical variable with a continuous variable: For example, we may be interested in knowing if the year in which a fight takes place (which is a categorical variable) has an effect on the average number of injuries fighters are likely to experience (which is a numeric continuous variable). Exhibit 4.2 in Chapter 4 provides an example of such an analysis. While it is obvious that the figures fluctuate from one year to the next, one needs to know how much of these fluctuations are due to randomness and how much can be attributed to true variations across the years. The method of analysis

used in such contexts is Analysis of Variance (ANOVA). This method produces multiple measures of statistical significance, and the one we will focus on here is the p value. This is similar to the p value used for Chi-square analysis described above, and with identical range and cut-off levels. The p value ranges from 0 to 1, and the closer it is to 0, the more significant the relationship. P values above 0.1 are typically not considered to be reflective of statistical significance.

(3) Relating two continuous variables: For example, we may be interested in knowing if the number of fights in which a fighter has participated is related to the method in which he typically wins fights. Exhibit 6.3 in Chapter 6 is an example of such a relationship. To determine if such a relationship is statistically significant and not due to randomness, we produce the Pearson Correlation. This figure ranges from -1 to +1. When it is close to 0, it indicates that there is no relationship between the two variables. When it is close to 1, it implies that for every one unit increase in one variable there is an increase of similar scale in the other variable. When it is close to -1, it indicates that for every unit of increase in one variable there is a decrease of similar scale in the other variable. Correlation analysis also produces a p-value similar to what was mentioned in the cases of Chi-square analysis and ANOVA, and the same cut-off values can be used to determine statistical significance.

(4) Predicting a categorical variable based on other categorical and continuous variables: For example, we may be interested in knowing if winning a fight (which is a categorical variable) is determined by a fighter's height and past win rates (both continuous variables) in addition to his age bracket and fighting stance (both categorical variables). The method of analysis used for such a situation is logistic regression. Logistic regression produces a predictive formula that relates the "dependent variable" (for example a fighter's win or loss) with a set of "independent variables," also called "predictors" (for example the fighter's height, age, past win rates and fighting stance). The discussion of the logistic regression methodology is beyond the scope of this book, and interested readers are encouraged to examine established sources on this topic.[3]

In the following chapters, a range of theories will be statistically tested in order to build a theoretical foundation for the drivers of combat outcomes in mixed martial arts competition. The above methods will be used throughout the chapters to test specific hypotheses. The accumulation of

---

[3] Two recommended resources are: Fred C. Pampel (2000), *Logistic Regression: A Primer*. Sage Publications, and Scott Menard (2001), *Applied Logistic Regression Analysis.* Sage Publications.

these hypothesis tests will enable us to build a foundational theory of combat success.

CHAPTER THREE

PATTERNS OF VICTORY IN MIXED MARTIAL ARTS COMBAT

In this chapter, we will examine the effects of the physical characteristics of fighters on fight outcomes. One of the foundations of combat theory in every martial arts style is that each combatant's physical characteristics affect his potential for winning a match. A combatant that is more physically fit than his opponent is assumed to be more likely to win, and physical fitness may itself be a function of a range of factors. For example, research in biology suggests that physical performance peaks at certain ages, and that age may be a determinant of performance measures in complex and challenging physical tasks.[4] While certain age ranges are more conducive to the development of new physical skills and growth in tissue cells, human physical performance declines beyond a certain age. This assertion can be observed in the context of tissue degradation reflected in muscle loss, neurological decay and an overall decline in endurance and physical reaction times in a range of competitive sports.[5]

In addition, research in sports medicine indicates that, in competitive sports, there is an increase in the number of injuries experienced by

---

[4] V. Bongard, A.Y. McDermott, G.E. Dallal, and E.J. Schaefer (2007), "Effects of Age and Gender on Physical Performance," *Age*, 29:77-85; J.L. Etnier and D.M. Landers (2005), "Motor Performance and Motor Learning as a Function of Age and Fitness," *Research Quarterly for Exercise and Sport*, , 11: 124-137; K.S. Nair (2005), "Aging Muscle," *American Journal of Clinical Nutrition*, 81: 953-93.
[5] B. Knechtle, C.A. Rust, T. Roseman and R. Lepers (2012), "Age-Related Changes in 100-km Ultra-Marathon Running Performance," *Age*, 34: 1033-1045; R. Lepers and T. Cattagni (2012), "Do Older Athletes Reach Limits in Their Performance During Marathon Running?," *Age*, 34: 773-781; B. Young and J. Starkes (2005), "Career-span Analyses of Track Performance: Longitudinal Data Present a More Optimistic View of Age-related Performance Decline," *Experimental Aging Research*, 31: 69-90.

athletes as their age increases.[6] In the context of combat sports, the probability of injury grows as one trains and competes more frequently. It can also increase with greater training intensity. An increase in the number of competitive fights contributes to increased probability of injuries experienced by an MMA fighter. Sustaining multiple injuries over the fighter's MMA career increases the likelihood of sustaining future injuries, and can deplete the athlete's ability to perform well as he ages.

In addition to age, the body size of a fighter may influence the likelihood of specific fight outcomes. For example, it is commonly believed that heavyweight fighters are less agile and, therefore, less capable of engaging in complex submission maneuvers. It is also often argued that, due to the greater amount of mass behind their strikes, heavier fighters are able to inflict greater physical damage to their opponents through striking. The validity of these commonly expressed theories can only be established through scientific examination of combat data.

---

[6] R. Bahr and L. Engebretsen (2009), *Handbook of Sports Medicine and Science, Sports Injury Prevention.* Wiley-Blackwell. See also Frederic Delavier and Michael Gundill (2013). *Delavier's Mixed Martial Arts Anatomy.* Human Kinetics.

In this chapter, the relationship between the physical characteristics of fighters and fight outcomes will be examined. Specifically, the effects of age and weight in determining fight outcomes will be studied. In the context of age, not only will we study the age of the fighter, but we will also examine the effects of age differences between the two opponents. Similarly, we will study how weight as well as weight differences between opponents affect fight conclusions. As will be shown in the analysis of the data, both of these physical conditions have systematic effects on fight outcomes.

Does Age Affect a Fighter's Ability to Win?

In order to examine the relationship between a fighter's age and fight outcomes, fighter age as well as the outcome of the fight were tabulated for each fighter in the Nevada State Athletic Commission data base (discussed in Chapter 2). Fighters' ages as provided by the Commission data used in this analysis ranged from 18 to 47 years old. The average age was 28.2 years[7]. In order to examine the relationship between age and fight outcomes, the percentage of fighters who experienced wins was computed for

---

[7] Only 1% of the fighters were 40 years old or older, and in order to enable the use of statistical methods, all analyses in this study are conducted on data for fighters between the ages of 18 and 39.

four specific age brackets. These percentages are shown in Exhibit 3.1.

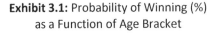

Exhibit 3.1: Probability of Winning (%) as a Function of Age Bracket

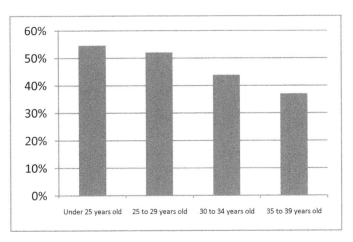

As can be seen from the exhibit, there is clearly an overall negative relationship between age bracket and the probability of winning. In the youngest age bracket (under 25 years old) a fighter has more than a 50/50 chance of winning. However, his chance of winning drops to nearly 1 in 3 for the 35-39 age bracket. This decline is steady, indicating a direct but negative relationship between aging and the likelihood of experiencing victory in competition. Statistical analysis on the data using Chi-square analysis indicates that the pattern observed in Exhibit 3.1 is statistically significant (p<.01, χ^2= 25.3; Φ

=0.104), suggesting that the results observed in the Nevada data will most likely replicate in similar settings, locations and fight contexts.

In order to further dissect the data and to determine at what age fighters peak in their win probabilities, the percentage frequency of wins was computed for each age (rather than age bracket). These frequencies are plotted in Exhibit 3.2. As can be seen, youthful fighters (e.g., 18 to 20 years old) have very low win probabilities. This is most likely attributed to lack of experience and training. However, fighters quickly peak such that the highest win probabilities are observed for 22 year old fighters. Fighter performance remains high until the age of 29, but then begins a steady decline. A rebound of fight performance occurs for fighters in their mid-30s, which may be a reflection of the buildup of experience level or recalibration of training in later stages of their professional careers, leading to enhanced win probabilities.

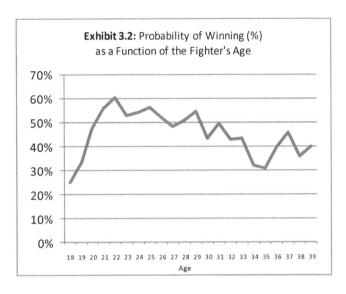

Exhibit 3.2: Probability of Winning (%) as a Function of the Fighter's Age

The overall results of this analysis suggest that age systematically depletes fighter performance. Furthermore, the results suggest that fighters peak in their win likelihood at the relatively early age of 22. In addition, as fighters age into their 30s, there is a dramatic drop in their probability of winning fights, such that 2 in 3 fighters in the 35-39 age category are likely to lose a fight.[8]

---

[8] It is important to note that these observations contrast with many of the traditionally held views on the relationship between age and fighter performance, which assume that fighters peak in later years. While such a proposition may be true in the context of more competitive venues (e.g., those promoted by the UFC,

Does Age Affect How a Fighter Wins?

While age seems to negatively influence a fighter's ability to win, it may assist the development of a more complete fighter. It is, therefore, possible that as fighters age and build experience, they develop new combat skills that enable them to execute more sophisticated techniques. For example, it is possible that more experienced fighters are able to end fights with submissions rather than decisions. In order to assess this proposition, an analysis was performed in order to determine the methods by which wins were achieved by all winning fighters. This data was then cross-tabulated with age in order to determine how age influences a winning fighter's method of finishing a fight.

Exhibit 3.3 provides a summary of how fights were finished. As can be seen, the most frequent fight ending was through a TKO (technical knockout) or a KO (knockout). Submissions account for about

---

Strikeforce, Bellator, etc.), in the general world of MMA fights (e.g., local shows and smaller promotions), younger fighters prevail according to the data. Fighters that survive the physical perils of age (which will be discussed in the next chapter) are the few that build up sufficient skills and experience to enter the more competitive venues and, therefore, evidence of an early peak observed in this study is not easily detectable for the major cards, which tend to recruit fighters with more fighting experience.

one third of all fight finishes. Decision wins occurred about 30% of the time. Less than one percent of wins occurred due to the disqualification of an opponent.

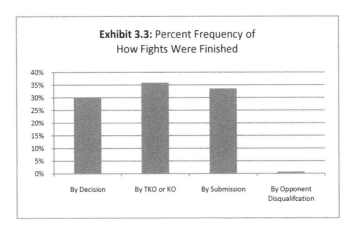

In order to examine if the above pattern varies by age, cross-tabulation was conducted between age brackets and the various methods of winning. This analysis is shown in Exhibit 3.4. The exhibit shows the method for how victory was usually achieved in each age bracket. For example, for fighters in the 35 to 39 age bracket, 22% of victories were achieved via submission and 48% via TKO or KO. As can be seen from the exhibit, the likelihood of achieving a win through KO or TKO significantly increases with age. This likelihood grows by nearly one-third between the youngest and oldest age brackets. In contrast, the likelihood of a win being achieved through a submission drops significantly with age.

Fighter's Age Bracket	Exhibit 3.4: How a Win is Achieved			
	Opponent Disqualification	Decision	TKO or KO	Submission
18 to 24	1.19%	29.76%	35.32%	33.73%
25 to 29	0.37%	30.57%	31.86%	37.20%
30 to 34	0.67%	29.29%	41.41%	28.62%
35 to 39	1.85%	27.78%	48.15%	22.22%

This finding contrasts with the theory that as fighters age, their ground-fighting techniques develop and they are increasingly able to finish fights through sophisticated methods such as submissions. Furthermore, the greater frequency of wins achieved through TKOs and KOs in higher age brackets contrasts with the view that age hinders the ability of fighters to rely on fighting methods dependent on fast reaction times. These results indicate that the use of striking to achieve wins in fact increases with age.[9] The differences across the age brackets observed in Exhibit 3.4 were tested using Chi-square analysis and found to be statistically significant (p<.05, χ^2=13.87; Φ =0.114).

---

[9] These results are also an outcome of variations in the training focus of younger versus older fighters. Older fighters have more experience with traditional fighting methods such as boxing and kickboxing, which have become less popular over the years with younger fighters as submission methods have grown in popularity with younger generations.

Does Being Younger Than the Opponent Affect One's Chances of Winning?

While the above results indicate that age can reduce the likelihood of winning, what happens when the opponents are not the same age? Is an older fighter more likely to win (perhaps due to greater fighting experience) or is he less likely to win (perhaps due to the physical effects of aging) against a younger opponent? To answer this question, the age difference between each fighter and his opponent was computed. Fighters were classified as being older than, younger than, or equal in age to their opponent in each match. For each of these three groups, win probabilities were then computed and are shown in Exhibit 3.5.

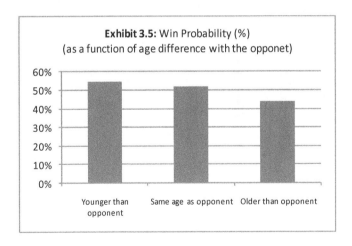

As can be seen from the exhibit, fighters who are younger than their opponents have a slight edge in terms of win probabilities. As expected, fighters who are older than their opponents have a reduced probability of winning a fight. These results concur with earlier analyses (e.g., Exhibit 3.2) that show the detrimental effect of aging on fight outcomes. To further dissect the above effects and to examine if the observed pattern becomes weaker or stronger depending on a fighter's age bracket, an additional analysis was conducted, and is shown in Exhibit 3.6.

Exhibit 3.6: Effects of Age Difference on Win Probabilities, by Age Bracket

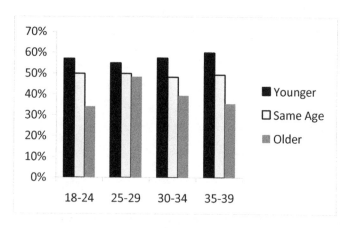

As can be seen from the exhibit, for a fighter in the lowest age bracket (18-24), being younger than the opponent significantly increases the fighter's win probability — increasing it to nearly 60%. This effect

is also evident for fighters in the oldest age range. Interestingly, the least effect for age difference is observed for fighters in the 25-29 age bracket. While being younger than one's opponent does improve one's odds of winning in this age bracket, the gain (relative to situations in which one is older than his opponent) is relatively minimal. These results further reinforce the effects of age, specifically in the context of age differences between opponents. Being older than one's opponent is consistently a disadvantage, which increases at higher age brackets.

Does Weight Class Affect How One Wins?

One of the central questions related to weight classes in mixed martial arts relates to how a fighter achieves victory. It is often assumed that lighter fighters are more agile and can, therefore, execute more complicated maneuvers compared to heavier fighters. In contrast, heavier fighters may be more damaging to their opponents when they strike (due to the greater mass supporting their strikes); as a result, they may be more effective in winning fights through knockouts. In order to determine the impact of weight class on how fights are won, the method of winning for all winning fighters was classified as being by decision, TKO (or KO), or submission. The data was then tabulated for each weight class and is shown in Exhibit 3.7.

Weight Class (pounds)	Exhibit 3.7: How Victory is Achieved (by Weight Class)		
	Won by Decision	Won by TKO or KO	Won by Submission
145 or less	38.36%	29.45%	32.19%
145 to 155	36.99%	23.74%	39.27%
156 to 170	29.64%	35.18%	35.18%
171 to 185	30.19%	35.85%	33.96%
186 to 205	26.63%	42.93%	30.43%
206 to 265	21.21%	53.03%	25.76%

As can be seen from the exhibit, the likelihood of achieving victory through a decision systematically declines at higher weight classes. For example, while over one third of the lighter fighters win through decisions, this number drops to less than one quarter for heavier fighters. At the same time, there is a systematic shift in how non-decision victories are achieved for different weight classes. Victory through TKO and KO becomes more likely for higher weight classes. In contrast, heavier fighters are less likely to win fights through submissions, as evident by a drop in the percentage of wins achieved through submission for higher weight classes. These results are consistent with the observation that fights in heavier weight classes are likely to result in more dramatic outcomes (as only about one quarter of heavy-weight fights are won by decision). Furthermore, combat styles such as Jiu jitsu and wrestling, which can effectuate submission wins, are more likely to be effective for lighter fighters who enjoy greater physical versatility. The differences in winning methods reported in Exhibit 3.7 across weight classes are statistically significant (p<.01; χ^2=44.14; Φ =0.195), and indicate that the results observed in the Nevada data will generalize to similar fight contexts elsewhere.

CHAPTER FOUR
PATTERNS OF INJURY IN MIXED MARTIAL ARTS COMBAT[10]

While the previous chapter focused on the impact of physical characteristics on a fighter's ability to win, this chapter will focus on data surrounding typical injuries that emerge from a fight. Given the combative nature of mixed martial arts, injuries

---

[10] This chapter is co-authored with Francis Dehel.

during a match are as expected an outcome as a win or a loss. Sanctioned mixed martial arts events organizers are required to provide on-site medical attention to fighters, and the events are to be supervised by medical professionals to ensure fighter safety. In addition, the injuries experienced by a fighter are documented by ringside physicians as part of the fight records released by sanctioning bodies such as state athletic commissions. The data captured from these records enables systematic analysis of the types of injuries experienced by fighters, as well as trends and correlates that contribute to injuries. In this chapter, the written reports provided by ringside physicians, as part of the Nevada State Athletic Commission data, are used to conduct this analysis.

How Many Injuries Do Fighters Typically Experience?

In order to examine the frequency of fighter injuries during competition, the post-fight medical reports for all injured fighters were analyzed. These reports provide detailed data on the types of injuries experienced by the fighter. This data was then subjected to content analysis procedures and categorized into 20 injury categories.[11] These categories were adopted from earlier studies in this research domain,[12] and include such injuries as facial lacerations, eye injuries, injuries to the arm, elbow and neck; they are detailed in Exhibit 4.1. In order to quantify the number of injuries experienced by a fighter, the total count of the number of injuries reported within these injury categories was computed for each fighter.

Analysis of the injuries documented for all the MMA fighters included in the data revealed the following: in 78% of the cases, no injuries were reported by the ringside physician; in less than 2% of all cases 3 or more injuries were reported. The average injury count across all fighters was 0.323. These injury patterns suggest an overall high degree of safety for fighters in mixed martial arts fights because, as revealed by the data, only about one in three fighters experienced any injury. However, injury counts were found to vary depending on the outcome of the fight. Winning fighters had an

---

[11] For additional details on content analysis procedures please consult K. Krippendorff (2012), *Content Analysis: An Introduction to its Methodology*. Sage Publications Inc.

[12] G.H. Bledsoe, E.B. Hsu, J.G. Grabowski, J.D. Brill and G. Li (2006), "Incidence of Injury in Professional Mixed Martial Arts Competitions," *Journal of Sports Science and Medicine*, 8: 136-142; K.M. Ngai, F. Levy and E.B. Hsu (2008), "Injury Trends in Sanctioned Mixed Martial Arts Competition: A 5-Year Review From 2002 to 2007," *British Journal of Sports Medicine*, 42: 686-689.

average injury count of 0.22. Losing fighters had an average injury count almost double that figure — an average injury count of 0.43. This difference is statistically significant (p<.01; t=58.8), and is an expected result since many fights (as reported in the previous chapter) are won not by decision but rather by knockouts or submissions, which can result in bodily damage to the losing fighter.

What Types of Injuries Do Fighters Experience?

In order to determine the nature of injuries experienced by fighters, a frequency tabulation of the injury categories was conducted. This analysis is shown in Exhibit 4.1. As can be seen from the exhibit, the most common forms of injury are facial lacerations. The second and third most common forms of injury are those related to the eyes and nose, respectively. All three injury types are typical of impact received due to striking techniques. Injuries to the arm, neck and elbow, are far less frequent. As these types of injuries are usually related to grappling and submission holds, this suggests that combatants utilizing techniques typical of submission fighting versus traditional styles of striking experience relatively safer outcomes.

Exhibit 4.1: Fighter Injury Frequencies by Injury Category

Type of Injury	Percent Frequency
Facial Laceration	9.05%
Eye	5.92%
Ear	0.30%
Nose	3.34%
Mouth	1.46%
Jaw	0.30%
Neck	0.00%
Shoulder	0.90%
Arm	0.47%
Elbow	1.11%
Hand	3.09%
Wrist	0.51%
Chest	0.47%
Abdomen	0.04%
Back	0.04%
Knee	1.37%
Ankle	0.51%
Foot	0.60%
Head	2.44%
Severe concussion	0.17%
Suspected Cervical Spine Injury	0.21%

Have Injury Rates Changed Over Time?

In order to determine if the average rate of injury has changed over time, average injury count figures were computed for each year of the study. One may expect that the rate of injury would decline over time due to increasingly strict regulations and added restrictions that prohibit specific attacks by fighters. In the early years of the sport, for example, kneeing a grounded opponent to the head was allowed; this form of strike has since become illegal. Similarly, head butts, downward elbow strikes from a top ground position, and pulling of the opponent's hair were allowed in the early days of MMA — moves that have all become illegal. To determine if the frequency of injuries has changed over the years, average injury count figures for each year are shown in Exhibit 4.2.

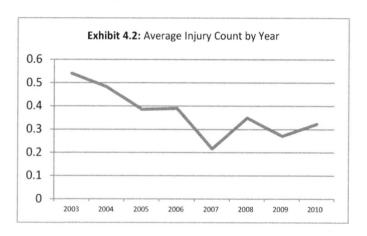

Exhibit 4.2: Average Injury Count by Year

As can be seen from the exhibit, there has been a general (though subtle) decline in the rate of injuries over time. The years 2003 and 2004 exhibited the highest injury counts, averaging about 0.5 per fighter. This means that, at that time, 5 out of every 10 fighters entering the cage were expected to receive a reportable injury by the end of the fight. The average injury count has gradually dropped over time, reaching a low of 0.2 in 2007. The changes over time in the average injury count were tested using Analysis of Variance, and are statistically significant ($p<.05$). Better refereeing of fights as well as enhancements in the defensive training of fighters may have helped reduce the likelihood of injuries over time. It is important however to recognize that the above analysis focuses on the frequency of injuries and not their severity. Ten (10) MMA events outside the scope of data used in this study have in fact resulted in death, many of which have occurred in recent years, and mostly in unsanctioned fights.

Does Age Affect the Number of Injuries Experienced During a Fight?

In order to determine if a fighter's age affects the likelihood of injury, average injury counts were computed for the four age brackets. These figures are plotted in Exhibit 4.3. As can be seen, there is a dramatic increase in the number of injuries above the age of 30. On average, fighters in their 30s experience 40% more injuries than fighters in their 20s. The differences across age brackets in terms of injury counts were tested using Analysis of Variance and are statistically significant ($p<.01$); they are also consistent with figures reported in the previous chapter relating to the drop in win likelihood for fighters in higher age brackets. The lower likelihood of victories for older fighters suggests that they are more susceptible to receiving injuries and that the two events (lower win rates and higher injury counts) may in fact be correlated.

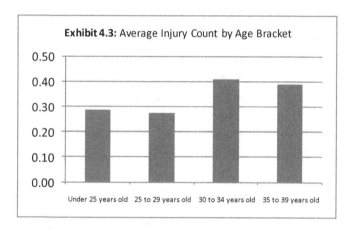

Exhibit 4.3: Average Injury Count by Age Bracket

Does the Difference Between Combatants' Ages Affect Injury Rates?

In addition to analyzing the statistically significant relationship between injury and a fighter's age, it is important to assess whether injuries experienced by a fighter may also relate to the age difference between the fighter and his opponent. As in the previous chapter, which focused on the effect of age difference between combatants on win probabilities, the difference between the age of each fighter and his opponent's age was computed in order to perform an analysis with relation to injuries experienced. The resulting age differences were then categorized into three groups: younger than the opponent, same age as the opponent, and older than the opponent. Average injury counts were then computed for each group and are reported in Exhibit 4.4.

As can be seen from the exhibit, fighters who are older than their opponents are significantly more likely to receive injuries when compared to those who fight opponents who are the same age or younger. The differences in injury counts across the different groups reported in Exhibit 4.4 were tested using Analysis of Variance; they are statistically significant (p<.01) and concur with the results of the previous chapter regarding win rate differences arising from differences in the ages of the fighters.

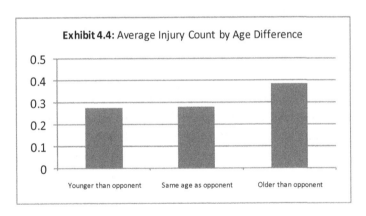

Does Weight Class Affect Injury Rates?

In order to determine if injury rates vary by weight class, average injury count figures were computed for each of the weight classes. These figures are shown in Exhibit 4.5.

Exhibit 4.5: Average Injury Count by Weight Class	
Weight Class (in pounds)	**Average Injury Count**
145 or less	0.275
146 to 155	0.289
156 to 170	0.359
171 to 185	0.314
186 to 205	0.342
206 to 265	0.360
Over 265	0.143

As can be seen from the exhibit, there appears to be a very subtle correlation between weight class and average injury count. For fighters below welterweight (156-170 pounds), the average injury count is below 0.3; for welterweight and heavier fighters, the average exceeds 0.3. However, the differences are subtle; for the most part, all weight classes experience similar frequencies of injuries. The only exception to this correlation is the over-265 pound category, in which lower rates of injuries seem to appear.[13] In contrast to age, which has been shown to have a direct relationship to injury rates, these results suggest that weight class is not strongly related to the rates of injuries experienced by MMA fighters.

---

[13] It is important, however, to note that the number of observations (fighters) in that weight class is small, and any differences observed are not statistically significant ($p > .1$).

CHAPTER FIVE
EFFECTS OF FIGHT CONTEXT ON FIGHT OUTCOMES

The previous two chapters focused on the effects of the physical characteristics of fighters on injuries and win rates. In this chapter, we will focus upon contextual variables. Context can significantly influence a fighter's state of mind. Many major MMA events draw hundreds, if not thousands of spectators and, in some cases, millions of pay-per-view audiences. Factors such as whether or not the fight takes place in the fighter's hometown or whether it is a title fight form the context of a fight. Such external elements impact the meaning of a win or loss for fighters, which affects their mental state although the technical foundations for what is physically needed to achieve victory inside the cage do not change.

Research in social psychology has suggested that the social setting in which individuals are asked to perform tasks has a direct influence on their performance.[14] In this chapter, several contextual variables will be studied in terms of their effects on the performance of MMA fighters as reflected by their win rates and method of winning. We will, for example, examine whether title fights result in different outcomes compared to non-title fights. In this chapter, we will also examine if the year in which a fight takes place relates to the method by which victory is achieved. We will also examine if the psychological pressure of waiting for a fight, as reflected by the order that a fight appears in the sequence of fights in a tournament, influences fight outcomes. In addition, we will examine whether fighter nationality affects win rates. For non-decision wins resulting from submissions or KO/TKO, an

---

[14] J. Dany, N. Brewer and R. Tottman (2001), "Self-Consciousness and Performance Decrements Within a Sporting Context," *Journal of Social Psychology*, 141: 150-152; M. Hagger and N. Chatzisarantis (2005), *The Social Psychology of Exercise and Sport*. Open University Press.

analysis will also be conducted to determine effects that the length of the fight may have had on the way in which the fight concluded.

Are Title Fights More Likely to Result in Non-Decision Conclusions?

Title fights create a tremendous amount of pressure on fighters. Not only are they often the main event featured in a tournament, but they are also closely scrutinized by the spectators and the media. Moreover, the risk of losing one's title or the prospects of gaining a title standing increase the motivation level of the opponents. The financial stakes associated with winning a title fight increase the fighters' desire to bring a conclusive end to a title fight, and to avoid leaving the decision to the judges.

A cross-tabulation analysis was conducted in order to determine if title fights are more likely to result in non-decision conclusions. The conclusion of each fight was noted, as well as whether or not it was a title fight. This cross-tabulation is shown in Exhibit 5.1. As can be seen from the exhibit, title fights are more likely to conclude with knockouts than non-title fights. In contrast, title fights are less likely to conclude with submissions or decisions. These results suggest that the added pressure and heightened psychological states surrounding title fights, as well as the skill sets brought into the cage by the combatants, increase the likelihood that title fights will conclude with knockouts. In contrast, for non-title fights, fighters tend to be more cautious; as a result, less dramatic endings, such as submissions and decisions, are more likely to prevail.

Exhibit 5.1: Non-Decision Fight Conclusions
(Title versus Non-title Fights)

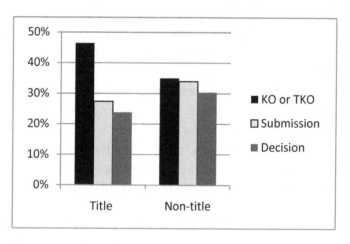

Does the Length of the Fight Influence the Outcome?

One of the tactical components of mixed martial arts is the ability to engage in multiple forms of attack on an opponent. Attacks can focus on strikes or submissions. However, a fighter's approach to attack may be influenced by the point during the fight at which the attack takes place. Early in a fight, there is little perspiration on fighters' bodies and the fighters demonstrate little fatigue. This may enable a fighter to secure a stronger grip on his opponent and, as a result, to more easily enable submission maneuvers to conclude a fight. However, as the fight progresses, due to the buildup of sweat on the skin and increased fatigue, submissions become more difficult to execute. It would be expected that, for fights that do not end in a decision, submission wins are more likely to occur earlier in the fight; as later rounds are reached, wins through striking become more likely. To test this proposition, we tabulated the round in which the fight ended for all fights that ended through a submission or knockout. This information is shown in Exhibit 5.2. As can be seen from the exhibit, fights that end in the first round are as likely to end by a knockout as they are to end by a submission. As the fight enters the 2nd and 3rd rounds, however, the likelihood of a win through a submission drops, eventually disappearing in championship rounds. This gives credence to the proposition outlined above: the effectiveness of submission techniques declines as fights progress through the rounds (χ^2=13.52; p<.01; Φ=0.135), especially when championship rounds (4 and 5) are reached.

Exhibit 5.2: Non-Decision Fight Conclusions
(as a Function of Conclusion Round)

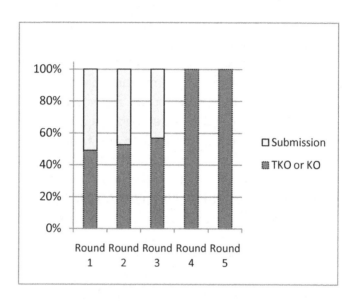

Does the Position on the Card Influence How a Fight Ends?

One of the variables included in the context of a fight is the position of the fight on the card in a given tournament. The mental state of a fighter whose fight is the first fight of the tournament may be different than it would be if his fight were later in the tournament. It is possible that fights that take place later in the tournament contribute to increased fighter anxiety, which may influence the way the fighters approach the fight. To examine this possibility, the order of the fight in the cards was matched against the way in which a fight concluded. This analysis is shown in Exhibit 5.3.

Exhibit 5.3: Effects of Position on the Card on Fight Conclusion			
Position on the Card	**Decision**	**KO or TKO**	**Submission**
First fight of the tournament	28.2%	31.9%	39.9%
2nd to 5th fight	29.3%	36.4%	34.3%
6th to 9th fight	31.5%	38.1%	30.5%
10th or higher	32.9%	34.3%	32.9%

As can be seen from the exhibit, there are no discernable relationships between the ways in which fights end and their position on the card. At first glance, it seems that submission wins are more likely in early fights, and that decision wins are more likely in later fights. However, the shift in the percentages reported are very subtle and do not reach statistically significant levels (χ^2=5.15; p=0.524; Φ=0.067). As a result, while one may postulate based on Exhibit 5.3 that fights early on a card are likely to end with submissions, this hypothesis can only be validated with more data as the existing data does not statistically support this proposition.

Have Fight Outcomes Evolved Over the Years?

The typical conclusions to fights may have evolved over time as fighter training has evolved and as promoters, referees and regulators become more attentive to fighter safety. As a result, it is possible that the manner in which fights conclude has evolved over the years. To examine this possibility, we examined fights within each year of the study and categorized conclusion methods into three major groups: decision, knockout (or TKO) and submission. The percentage frequency of these categories was then computed for every year. This analysis is shown in Exhibit 5.4.

Exhibit 5.4: Method of Fight Conclusion by Year

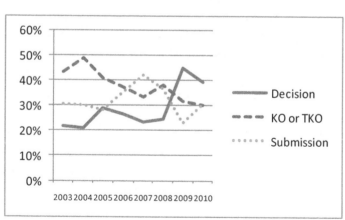

As can be seen from the exhibit, there has been a clear evolution over time in terms of how fights conclude. While, in the early years of the study, only about one in five fights ended with a decision, this figure nearly doubled by the end of the study period. This trend may reflect fighters' gradually improved ability to defend themselves against strikes and submission attempts, which would result in non-decision finishes. The exhibit further demonstrates that the percentage frequency of fights ending with a knockout, which had reached nearly 50% in the earlier years of this study, significantly and consistently dropped over the years. This also may be a result of the maturation of the field and improved fighter training for defense against strikes.

Are Fighters From Certain Countries Better than Others?

It is often observed that there are differences in the training programs of fighters across the world.[15] Brazil, for example, was one of the pioneering countries in promoting and establishing mixed martial arts. There is a long history of mixed martial arts combat in Brazil, dating to the early parts

---

[15] Clyde Gentry (2011), *No Holds Barred: The Complete History of Mixed Martial Arts in America.* Triumph Books. See also B.J. Penn, Glen Cordoza, and Erich Krauss (2007). *Mixed Martial Arts: The Book of Knowledge.* Victory Belt Publishing.

of the previous century and the traditions of Vale Tudo. Grappling and submission methods are very popular among MMA practitioners in this country. Fighters from Europe and Asia, in contrast, often receive training in kickboxing and Muay Thai. American fighters' strength, on the other hand, is often assumed to be in wrestling and boxing. These nationally-driven differences in training programs may affect a fighter's performance in a mixed martial arts setting.

In order to determine if differences exist in the probability of a fighter winning depending on his country of origin, win percentages were computed for each country/region. These are shown in Exhibit 5.5. It appears that Brazilian fighters have a slight edge over fighters from other countries, and that fighters from Asia are less effective. The differences are minor and, in fact, from a statistical point of view, do not reach significant levels ($\chi^2=1.88$; p=0.757; $\Phi=0.028$). The lack of statistical significance indicates that additional data would be needed to support or refute the proposition that cross-country variations exist in fighter abilities. The existing data does not indicate that any such differences exist.

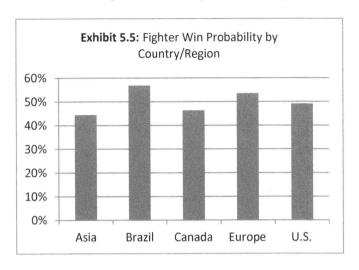

Exhibit 5.5: Fighter Win Probability by Country/Region

Is There a Hometown Advantage?

There is one common question in any competitive event: Is there a hometown advantage? Competitors from the area in which the event is being held are likely to experience more fan support. Furthermore, the accessibility of their training facilities expedites their preparations. In contrast, out-of-town fighters must travel to the event location and may experience travel fatigue, jet lag, and other inconveniences with which hometown fighters do not have to contend. To determine if hometown fighters have an advantage, win frequencies were computed for fighters from the same home state (Nevada) and for those fighters who were traveling from out of state. These figures are reported in Exhibit 5.6.

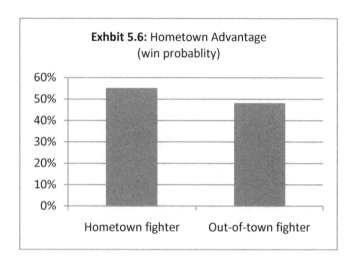

As can be seen from the exhibit, hometown fighters have a distinct advantage over out-of-town fighters. Their likelihood of winning fights is approximately 10% higher than their out-of-town opponents. This difference is statistically significant (χ^2=5.96; p<.01; Φ=0.051) and supports the proposition that there is a hometown advantage in MMA competitions. It is, however, important to acknowledge that, while some of this advantage may be attributed to fighting in one's home state, in this particular case it may also be due to the superior performance of fighters from the state of Nevada, where many great MMA academies reside.

CHAPTER SIX
THE FIGHTER VERSATILITY INDEX

$$FVI = \frac{\dfrac{0.333}{\overline{WKO^2+WSUB^2+WDEC^2}} - 0.333}{0.666}$$

One of the fundamental characteristics of mixed martial arts competition is the ability of the fighters to utilize a variety of techniques to overcome their opponents. The techniques could include striking (kicks, punches, knee strikes, etc.), submissions (arm bars, choke holds, etc.) or takedowns. In the ideal circumstance for any fighter, the use of these techniques would result in the early termination of the fight through knockout or submission of his opponent or stoppage by the referee. If a fight completes its time limit, the use of these techniques would result in the accumulation of points scored by ringside judges for each opponent, and the rendering of a decision by the judges at the end of the time limit of the fight. The decision would be in favor of the fighter with the greater number of accumulated points.

Each fighter has a preference for the types of techniques he uses in the cage. Some fighters prefer to use striking while others rely more on grappling methods. Fighters also vary in the way they win fights. Some are able to finish fights before the end of the fight's time limit, for example by submitting their opponents; others will prolong the fight to the end of the time limit, at which point a decision is rendered by the judges. The propensity to win fights in various ways (knockout, submission or decision) is a central characteristic of every fighter and varies from one fighter to the next. The accumulation of detailed win and loss data for fighters as they advance in their professional careers provides a dynamic picture of evolving fighter characteristics. These characteristics can be quantified, as will be shown in this chapter, to establish a measure of the degree of versatility that a fighter possesses.

Data Source

In order to quantify fighter versatility, professional fight records for 146 MMA fighters who had completed fights between May 1996 and May 2013 were compiled. For each fighter, official detailed fight records for each professional event in which he had competed were used. The records include data on the result (e.g., win, loss, draw, etc.) and the method by which the result was reached (e.g., knockout, submission, etc.) This data is openly accessible on the Internet from a variety of sources and can be used to obtain a detailed picture of a fighter's combat history.

Computing Win and Loss Ratios

In order to enumerate the unique characteristics of each fighter, a series of ratios can be computed. These include the ratio of wins through knockouts (WKO), ratio of wins through submissions (WSUB), ratio of wins through decisions (WDEC), ratio of losses by knockouts (LKO), ratio of losses by submissions (LSUB) and ratio of losses by decisions (LDEC). These ratios quantify the extent of effectiveness of the fighter through specific approaches to combat as well as his vulnerabilities resulting from specific weaknesses, which have resulted in losses. They are described in more detail below:

WKO = Percent of wins achieved through knockouts (or TKOs); the greater this number, the more likely the fighter is to win a fight through striking and ground-and-pound methods.

WSUB = Percent of wins achieved through submissions; the greater this number, the more likely the fighter is to submit his opponents.

> WDEC = Percent of wins achieved through decisions; the greater this number, the more likely the fighter is to win a fight through the judges' decision.

The ratios related to losses represent mirror images of the corresponding win ratios and are outlined below:

> LKO = Percent of losses experienced through knockouts or TKOs

> LSUB = Percent of losses experienced through submissions

> LDEC = Percent of losses experienced through decisions

In the above computations, wins and losses due to disqualification, no contest and draws are omitted to simplify the analysis, as cases of fights ending with these outcomes accounted for less than 3% of all fight outcomes. It is important to point out that the above measures are dynamic and change for each fighter as he progresses through his professional career. Exhibit 6.1 provides an example of how these ratios are computed, using a numeric example for a hypothetical fighter.

Exhibit 6.1: An Example of Ratio Calculations

	Fight Outcome	WKO	WSUB	WDEC	LKO	LSUB	LDEC
First fight	Won by KO	1.00	0.00	0.00	0.00	0.00	0.00
Second fight	Won by decision	0.50	0.00	0.50	0.00	0.00	0.00
Third fight	Lost by submission	0.50	0.00	0.50	0.00	1.00	0.00
Fourth fight	Lost by submission	0.50	0.00	0.50	0.00	1.00	0.00
Fifth fight	Won by KO	0.66	0.00	0.33	0.00	1.00	0.00
Sixth fight	Won by decision	0.50	0.00	0.50	0.00	1.00	0.00
Seventh fight	Lost by submission	0.50	0.00	0.50	0.00	1.00	0.00
Eighth fight	Won by decision	0.40	0.00	0.60	0.00	1.00	0.00

The example provided in Exhibit 6.1 is for a hypothetical fighter as he advances through his career. In his very first fight, he achieved victory through a knockout. At that point in time, the only victory he experienced was the one knockout he had achieved; therefore, the computed value for WKO is 1.0. However, in his next fight, he won by decision. At that point in time, half (1 of 2) of his victories came through a knockout and the other half through a decision; therefore, the values for WKO and WDEC are both 0.5. He lost his next two fights but won his fifth fight by knockout. After his 5th fight, of the 3 victories he had, 2 were achieved by knockout and one by decision, making the values for WKO and WDEC 0.66 and 0.33, respectively. The same logic can be used to visualize how loss ratios (LKO, LSUB and LDEC) are computed.

The above analysis shows how fighter characteristics evolve over time. For the fighter profiled in Exhibit 6.1, for example, wins were likely to occur through knockouts toward the beginning of his professional career; toward the end, however, he became more likely to achieve wins through decisions. Furthermore, the data reveals that this fighter was unable to win fights through submissions (as the WSUB figure is consistently equal to 0). In addition, all of his losses have come through submissions as the LSUB figure is at 1.0 and none of the other loss ratios (LKO and LDEC) are greater than 0.

This analysis suggests that this fighter is at great risk of losing fights due to submissions and is unlikely to win fights through submissions. Such an observation can provide prescriptive directions for effective training programs, especially when conducting a similar analysis for the fighter he is about to face in an upcoming fight. For example, if the next fighter he will be facing is known to win the majority of his fights through submissions (for example has a WSUB ratio of 0.8), there is a great risk of a submission loss and training needs to focus on submission defense. Examining the ratios also allows one to observe how fights typically end and to understand the variety of methods through which fighters achieve victory or experience defeat.

What are Typical Win and Loss Ratios?

In order to determine typical win and loss ratios, average figures were estimated for the fighters profiled in the data set. These figures are shown in Exhibit 6.2. Since fighters vary in terms of their win ratios — for example, with some more likely to win by submissions and some more likely to win by way of knockouts — it is important to be able to group them into different categories. Therefore, a statistical method called cluster analysis was used to group fighters into the various subgroups.[16] This method allows the win ratios to be used as inputs to classify a fighter into one of 3 fighter types: strikers (those who tend to win through knockouts or TKOs), submitters (those who tend to win using submissions) and decision winners (those who typically win by decision).

---

[16] A recommended resource for understanding the cluster analysis methodology is: J.F. Hair, W.C. Black, B.J. Babin, and R. E. Anderson (2010). *Multivariate Data Analysis.* Upper Saddle River: Prentice Hall.

Exhibit 6.2: Average Win Ratios by Fighter Type

	WKO	WSUB	WDEC
Strikers	**0.627**	0.222	0.144
Submitters	0.228	**0.635**	0.126
Decision Winners	0.232	0.244	**0.442**
Sample Strikers			
Johnny Hendricks	**0.639**	0.121	0.239
John Jones	**0.659**	0.218	0.123
Anderson Silva	**0.609**	0.145	0.246
Sample Submitters			
Kenny Florian	0.383	**0.577**	0.040
Frank Mir	0.115	**0.634**	0.251
Antonio Rodrigo Nogueira	0.055	**0.763**	0.182
Sample Decision Winners			
Rashad Evans	0.345	0.193	**0.462**
Dan Henderson	0.451	0.053	**0.495**
Lyoto Machida	0.345	0.119	**0.535**

Based on this analysis, 38% of fighters would be classified as strikers, 42% as submitters and 20% as decision winners. Exhibit 6.2 shows the average win ratios for these fighters as well as ratios for the other two categories of fighters based on fighter categorization obtained through cluster analysis. It is important to note that classifying a fighter as belonging to one of these groups does not imply that the fighter is not able to achieve victory through other means; rather, he is more likely to win by the method in which he is classified. To demonstrate this, in Exhibit 6.2 win ratios are provided for some of the most well-known fighters in the sport.

How Do Win Ratios Change Over Time?

In order to examine if the win and loss ratios change as fighters gain more fighting experience, ratio computations were conducted for various points in the fighters' careers. These figures are shown Exhibit 6.3.

Exhibit 6.3: Average Fighter Ratios

	WKO	WSUB	WDEC
Fifth fight	0.399	0.432	0.169
Tenth fight	0.383	0.422	0.195
Twentieth fight	0.382	0.383	0.235

As can be seen from Exhibit 6.3, win ratios evolve over time. While variations exist in how fighters typically win fights in the early stages of their careers, their methods of winning become more diverse as they mature. By the twentieth fight, the ratios are nearly equal for knockouts (WKO) and submissions (WSUB). Furthermore, the win ratio for decisions systematically grows over time. This demonstrates that fighters may become more risk-averse and opt for a conservative approach such as winning by points (decision) over the course of their careers; this may explain the growth over time of the WDEC ratio. Correlation analysis confirms the above observations, as the likelihood of a win achieved by a decision increases with fighter experience (correlation =0.116; p<0.01).

Can Fighter Versatility Be Quantified?

One of the defining characteristics of a fighter is his versatility, as reflected by the ability to utilize various approaches in order to achieve victory. Fighters that lack versatility are one dimensional and, while they may be excellent at specific skills, they may lack important skills in other areas. For example, a fighter who is a good striker but is unable to execute submissions or defend against them is not viewed as highly versatile. The win and loss indices discussed earlier in this chapter can be used to quantify fighter versatility. Versatility measures can be computed using a widely established index called the Herfindhal index, commonly used for strategic analysis in competitive settings such as business, market competition, industry alliances and warfare.[17]

---

[17] D. Aaker (2009), *Strategic Market Management*. Wiley; B. Chevalier-Riognant and L. Trigeorgis (2009), *Competitive Strategy: Options and Games.* MIT Press.

In the context of the win measures discussed earlier, the Herfindhal index can be computed as such:

$$Herfindhal\ Index = WKO^2 + WSUB^2 + WDEC^2$$

To demonstrate the characteristics of the Herfindhal index, a sample computation is provided in Exhibit 6.4.

Exhibit 6.4: Sample Herfindhal Index and FVI Computations

	WKO	WSUB	WDEC	Herfindhal Index	Fighter Versatility Index
Fighter A	1.00	0.00	0.00	1.000	0.000
Fighter B	0.90	0.10	0.00	0.820	0.109
Fighter C	0.25	0.25	0.50	0.375	0.833
Fighter D	0.33	0.33	0.33	0.333	1.000

As can be seen from the exhibit, fighter A is a one-dimensional fighter. He achieves all wins through knockouts (WKO=1.00) and has not achieved victory through any other means. The computed Herfindhal index for fighter A is 1.0. Fighter B is a bit less rigid and is also able to execute submissions, which he does rarely, as well as win through knockouts; based on his win ratio figures, the computed Herfinhal index for this fighter is 0.82. Fighter C is even more versatile and fighter D exhibits the greatest level of versatility. Fighter D is able to win through all three approaches with equal likelihood.

Fighter D represents a highly balanced fighting style — one that enables the achievement of victory through a variety of means. For the unique state of equal likelihood of achieving a win through the various possible means, the Herfindhal index is 0.333. This figure is the lowest level that the Herfindhal can be for such a context. Therefore, the most flexible (least rigid) scenario is demonstrated by Fighter D, and the associated figure for the Herfindhal index can be used as a baseline to quantify versatility levels for all fighters. To quantify a fighter's level of versatility, the figure 0.333 can be divided by the Herfindhal index for a given fighter. Once it has been re-scaled to be a figure between 0 and 1 (as shown in the equation below), it can be easily used as a basis of comparison for the versatility levels of competing fighters. This figure is shown in the rightmost column of Exhibit 6.4 and will be referred to as the Fighter Versatility Index (FVI) in the balance of this book:

$$FVI = \frac{\frac{0.333}{WKO^2 + WSUB^2 + WDEC^2} - 0.333}{0.666}$$

FVI ranges from a low of 0 to a high of 1. The higher the FVI, the more versatile is the fighter. A high figure indicates that the fighter is capable of achieving wins through a variety of means.

What Are Typical Versatility Levels for Fighters?

The lowest value that FVI can take is 0. This situation reflects the lowest level of versatility. The highest level that FVI can possibly take is 1, reflecting the greatest degree of versatility. For the sample of fighters used in this chapter, the average FVI figure was found to be 0.615. As indicated by earlier analyses presented in this chapter, the range of methods by which fighters achieve victory expands as they advance through their careers. This should result in improvements in the fighter versatility index. To explore this possibility and to identify the rate of growth, a plot of FVI versus the number of fights in a fighter's history was produced. This is shown in Exhibit 6.6. As can be seen from the exhibit, there is an evolutionary growth in FVI levels as fighters progress in their careers as indicated by the number of fights (x-axis). Significant increases are witnessed during the first six fights, after which the growth in the versatility index slows down.

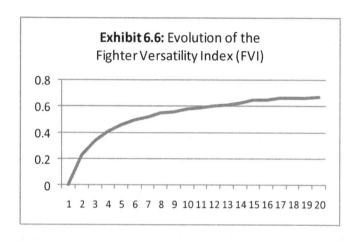

Exhibit 6.6: Evolution of the Fighter Versatility Index (FVI)

Does a Loss Lead to a Win in the Next Fight?

One of the questions that often emerges in competitive sports is how a loss impacts an athlete's desire and drive to perform better in the next event. Research in psychology has shown that losses have a great impact on human psychology and motivation when compared to wins[18]. The emotional and cognitive effects of a loss in a competitive setting may be the driving force that motivates a fighter to improve his training, develop skills in areas in which he was lacking, and to reexamine the circumstances

---

[18] Amos Tversky and Daniel Kahneman (1981), "The Framing of Decisions and the Psychology of Choice," *Science,* Vol. 211, pp. 453-463; Max H. Bazerman (2002), *Judgment in Managerial Decision Making.* John Wiley and Sons: New York; H. Shefrin and M. Statman (1985), "The Disposition to Sell Winners Too Early and Ride Losers Too Long: Theory and Evidence," *Journal of Finance,* Vol. 40, pp. 777-790.

leading to an unprepared state resulting in a loss. In the context of mixed martial arts competitions, it is very important to ensure that consecutive losses do not occur; two or three losses in a row may result in the fighter being eliminated from consideration by matchmakers in the future. Because of this, it is possible that fighters who have experienced a loss in their previous fight have greater motivation to win the next fight. To test this proposition, a cross-tabulation was done to determine a fighter's likelihood of winning a given fight as a function of the outcome of his previous fight. Exhibit 6.7 provides a visual display of this relationship.

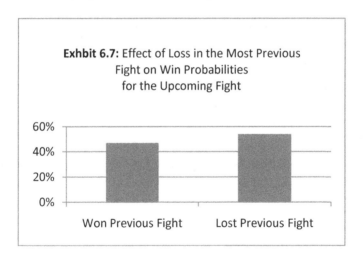

As can be seen from the exhibit, a loss in the previous fight significantly increases the probability of winning the next fight. The win probability increases by nearly 10% when one is coming off of a loss. This difference is statistically significant (χ^2=4.76; p<.05; Φ=-0.07) and testifies to the strong drive of a fighter who has just experienced a loss in his previous fight.

Do Early Signs of Fighter Success Exist?

While the above analysis showed that having experienced a loss in the most recent fight increases the likelihood of a fighter winning his next fight, one may also ask if early wins (those in the few first professional fights of a fighter) are predictive of success over the fighter's career. The examination of the profile of a fighter beginning with his first fight until the most recent of his fights may reveal a pattern of wins and losses that provides an indication of these capabilities. One interesting pattern that is evident in the history of many top fighters is that those who excel to the top of the sport — for example, those who gain championship status or become contenders — typically did extremely well in the early stages of their careers as professional fighters.

To further examine the above observation, fighters were grouped into two categories: those who had never experienced a loss in their first 5 professional MMA fights and those that had experienced at least one loss in their first 5 fights. Win probabilities for subsequent fights (6th and above) each of these two groups were then computed. This is shown in Exhibit 6.8.

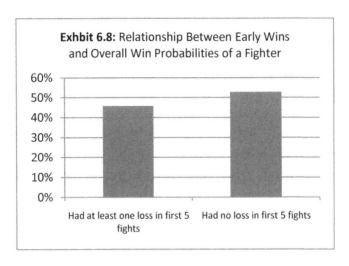

Exhbit 6.8: Relationship Between Early Wins and Overall Win Probabilities of a Fighter

As can be seen from the exhibit, fighters who had a perfect early record (had no losses in their first 5 fights) generally have higher win rates in the fights following the first five fights. The differences in the win rates between the two groups are statistically significant (χ^2=4.32; p<.05; Φ=-0.07). These results indicate that signs of a great fighter may be apparent in early fights.

Does Experience Give a Fighter an Advantage?

When comparing the relative strengths of two fighters, one of the variables that is often cited is the difference in the experience levels of the fighters. It is often assumed that fighters who have more experience than their opponents, as measured by the number of professional fights over their careers, are more likely to win. To determine if this is the case, all fighters who had at least 6 fights in their professional MMA records were grouped into three categories in this analysis: those with experience levels equal to their opponents (within ± 3 professional fights); those who are more experienced (have had 4 or more fights than their opponents); and those that are less experienced (fall short of their opponents by 4 or more fights). Exhibit 6.9 shows the pattern of results.

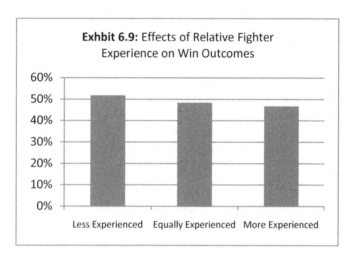

Exhbit 6.9: Effects of Relative Fighter Experience on Win Outcomes

As can be seen from the exhibit, the effects of experience seem to oppose the expected outcome related to the likelihood of winning a fight. More experienced fighters seem to have a lower probability of winning. This relationship can be explained by the fact that more experienced fighters are often older and, as outlined in detail in Chapter 3, age has a diminishing effect on win probabilities. Furthermore, with more professional fights come more injuries, which may impact a fighter's performance or his ability to train for an upcoming fight. It is important to note that, although interesting, the pattern does not reach significance from a statistical perspective (χ^2=1.57; p=0.45; Φ=-0.04). The lack of statistical significance may be due to the fact that the quality of opponents is not captured in this measure, making the experience level of a fighter as measured by the number of professional fights he has had a highly unreliable measure. A fighter may have accumulated a large number of fights, but if the opponents he has faced were not challenging, experience will not be an accurate measure of his combat capabilities.

What Other Fighter Performance Measures Exist?

In addition to the measures discussed in this chapter, which reflect a fighter's history of fighting and quantify how wins and losses were experienced by a fighter, other measures can be quantified in order to reflect a fighter's capabilities when entering the cage. These include the average speed through which a fighter is typically able to bring a fight to a decisive end (for example fighters that knock out their opponents within 2 minutes of the first round), and the percentage of previous fights that have ended in non-decision wins (for example, 80% of fights won by knockouts or submission). In addition to a fighter's fighting experience, the physical features of the fighter (for example, age, height and reach), some of which were discussed in the previous chapters and some of which will be detailed in the next chapter, can have a profound impact on fight outcomes. Clearly, a fighter's performance is also affected by his training discipline as well as his state of mind when entering the cage. Some of these variables will be discussed in Chapter 9.

CHAPTER SEVEN
THE EFFECTS OF FIGHTER HEIGHT AND REACH

In the early days of mixed martial arts, regulations were not put in place to monitor the body sizes of opposing fighters chosen to fight in a match. Fighters of significantly different sizes could be facing each other inside the cage. This, in fact, was one of the early attractions of the sport; it not only reflected the more typical scenarios representative of street fights, but it also tested the limits and effectiveness of many traditional forms of combat by pitting smaller fighters against larger opponents. Many MMA fans and fighters vividly recall the scenes of the earliest fights in UFC1 when Royce Gracie overcame his larger opponents. The ability of a small fighter to submit his larger opponent was one of the main driving forces behind the early growth and popularity of mixed martial arts.

Interestingly, many of the fighters who subsequently entered the cage after Royce Gracie found that size difference can in fact be a challenge difficult to overcome. Size disparity between fighters often creates unbalanced combat scenarios favoring the larger fighters. Few fighters with the ground skills and experience level of Royce Gracie could manage to overpower their larger opponents. As a result, encouraged by regulators, the sport has transitioned toward regulating fighter size. This regulation utilizes a system based upon weight classes. Fighters are weighed in advance of fights, often a day in advance, to ensure that their body weight does not exceed the limits set for the weight class in which they compete. Fighters who are outside the weight limit are often financially penalized and, in some cases, their opponents can choose not to fight them.

The classification of fighter size through weight is a common practice in many combat sports including boxing, kickboxing and wrestling. Since MMA fighters are able to execute a much wider array of attacks against their opponents as compared to traditional combat sports, an emerging question is whether or not using the same classification system for fighter size is appropriate for mixed martial arts. The process of managing, controlling, and cutting weight has become a science and a pre-fight ritual that may pose medical risks for fighters who have to cut a significant amount of weight. The practice also allows fighters of much larger frame who are able to cut weight to be matched against opponents of smaller frame sizes. Weight cuts in the range of 30 to 50 pounds to achieve entry into the cage as a lighter fighter are not atypical, and are often achieved through starvation diets and dehydration routines.

A question emerging from the above observation relates to whether measures of body size other than weight can help classify fighters or predetermine their ability to succeed in MMA competition. We will examine the effects of two other measures that describe the body frame of a fighter, namely reach and height. Reach reflects the length of the arms and a fighter's ability to strike his opponent at greater distances. Height reflects the vertical advantage that a fighter may have, which may make it easier for him to strike critical targets (such as the head and neck) on his opponent's body. Using a combination of fight record data and fighter frame measures, we will examine over the course of this chapter the impact that reach and height might have on the probability of winning fights.

What Are Typical Fighter Frame Sizes?

There are significant variations in fighter frame size across fighters. It is not uncommon to have a fighter who is well over 6 feet tall compete as a lightweight fighter (maximum weight of 155 pounds), or to have a fighter with the frame of a typical lightweight fight in welter-weight (170 pound weight limit) or even middle-weight (185 pound limit) bouts. Understanding the average figures for fighter frames may be informative. Publicly available data were obtained on the height and reach of the fighters for whom fight records were extracted for use in the data set analyzed in the previous chapter. The average height of fighters was found to be 5'11". Fighter height ranged from a low of 5'3" to a high of 7'. These figures demonstrate the popularity of the sport and its ability to accommodate a wide range of body sizes.

With respect to reach, the average figure was found to be 73 inches. In the data used in this analysis, reach ranged from a low of 66 inches to a high of 84.5 inches. To better describe the frame of a fighter, another relevant measure is the ratio of a fighter's reach divided by his height. The average for this ratio was found to be 1.03, and it ranged from a low of 0.96 to a high of 1.11.

Do Frame Size Differences Influence Win Rates?

Reach and height can have meaningful implications on fight strategy and resulting outcomes. Reach represents the distance at which a fighter can strike his opponent. It can also represent how far he can fend off an opponent in order to prevent takedowns or other forms of attack. It is, therefore, important not only to look at a fighter's reach, but also to examine how his reach compares to that of his opponent. Similarly, height differences may provide taller fighters with a tactical advantage since a height advantage may make it easier for a taller fighter to strike the head of his shorter opponent.

To examine the potential role that differences between fighters in terms of height and reach may have on fight outcomes, fighters were classified into various categories based on the difference between their height and reach and that of their opponents. Exhibit 7.1 contains the results of this analysis and relates reach differences with the probability of winning a fight. As can be seen from the exhibit, there is a direct relationship between reach advantage and probability of winning. Fighters whose reach is within 3.5 inches of the reach of their opponent have an equal likelihood of winning or losing the fight. However, a reach disadvantage reduces the likelihood of winning to less than 1 in 3, and as expected, an opposite effect occurs with a reach advantage in excess of 3.5 inches. The differences observed were tested using Chi-square analysis and found to be statistically significant (p<.01, χ^2= 12.5; Φ =0.2).

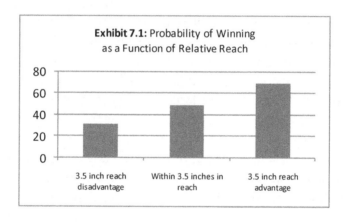

The results of Exhibit 7.1 testify to the great impact that reach has on fight outcomes. In fact, when examining the average reach differences for some of the most well-known MMA champions, notable reach advantages over opponents are observed. A sample of these figures is provided in Exhibit 7.2. The figures demonstrate the average reach advantage enjoyed by these fighters across all their professional MMA fights. As can be seen from the exhibit, these fighters have enjoyed an obvious tactical advantage over their opponents. This advantage may be a function of two distinct yet related elements: being matched against opponents who have a reach disadvantage, and the winners' exceptional body frame. The body frames of such iconic fighters as Jon Jones and Anderson Silva, for example, provided them with extraordinary reach which had helped them secure a tactical advantage over most of their opponents.

Exhibit 7.2: Average Reach Advantage for Champions (in inches)

Jon Jones	9.75
Anderson Silva	4.24
Georges St. Pierre	2.70
Nick Diaz	4.67
Matt Hughes	2.67

To further explore the question of frame size differences, a similar analysis was conducted for differences between the heights of the combatants. This analysis is shown in Exhibit 7.3. As can be seen from the exhibit, there is a direct and very strong effect of height difference on the probability of a win for a particular fighter. Shorter fighters are at a significant disadvantage, such that a height disadvantage of over 4 inches can translate into a winning probability of less than 1 in 5. These differences, tested using Chi-square analysis, were found to be statistically significant ($p<.01$, $\chi^2= 9.9$; $\Phi =0.18$).

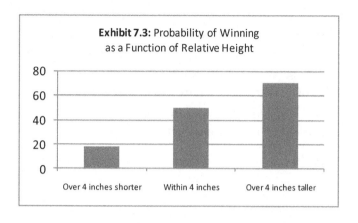

Exhibit 7.3: Probability of Winning as a Function of Relative Height

How Do Advantages in Reach and Height Influence the Method of Winning?

The results shown above indicate that differences in frame size between combatants can directly affect fight outcomes. The probability of winning drastically improves with reach and height advantages. Additional analyses were conducted in order to assess whether frame size differences influence how a fight is won. The results show that a 4 inch height advantage for one fighter over the other in a match can increase the probability of a submission win 3-fold compared to situations in which height differences are within 4 inches. A similar 3-fold increase in the likelihood of submission wins is observed when a reach advantage of 3.5 inches or more is enjoyed by a fighter. Reach and height advantages help keep opponents at bay when the fight is on the feet. When a fight moves to the ground, these advantages make it easier for a larger fighter to execute submission maneuvers and to gain physical control of his smaller opponent. Interestingly, neither height advantage nor reach advantage influence the likelihood of knockout wins at statistically significant levels. These results suggest that frame size can be a predictor of a win — be it by submission, knockout or decision — rather than a predictor that victory in the cage will be achieved by a certain type of maneuver. The findings are practically significant, however, in that they challenge the validity of weight classes. Fighter frame characteristics seem to drastically influence fight outcomes to a more significant extent than previously recognized. This puts into question the validity of fighter weight as the basis for classification of fighters and requires promoters and regulators to examine the possibility of creating more balanced fight cards using frame size as a basis for matching fighters.

Does the Fighter's Stance Influence Fight Outcomes?

Modeling themselves after traditions and norms in boxing, MMA fighters often have a preferred stance. This means that fighters either prefer to fight with their left arm leading the body (called an orthodox stance) or with their right arm leading the body (called a southpaw stance). In contrast, fighters are trained to fight in both stances in many traditional forms of martial arts such as

Karate and Kung Fu. Over the years, the fast pace of movement in MMA and boxing fights has encouraged fighters to take on either an orthodox or southpaw stance, and to remain with that stance during the majority of their combat engagement. Very few fighters are fully versatile and comfortable with switching stances mid-fight.

Of the fighters profiled in this study, 76% used an orthodox stance. This is expected since most individuals are right handed and would by default prefer to reserve their power punch to the right hand, causing them to lead with their left hand. The remaining 24% of fighters who are primarily southpaw can confuse the majority of their opponents (the 76% of fighters who are not southpaw). Since the majority of fighters have an orthodox stance, few are able to experience fighting a southpaw fighter during training. Fighting in a southpaw stance against an orthodox fighter allows the southpaw to use the left roundhouse high kick to the head, and also to circle to the left of the orthodox opponent in order to punch the opponent outside his immediate striking range. Some southpaw fighters may be able to take better advantage of this stance than others, as it often requires a greater reach when circling to the left side of the opponent or greater height in order to land the head kick using the left foot. To assess this proposition, average height and reach figures were estimated for southpaw versus orthodox fighters and are shown in Exhibit 7.4. As evident from the exhibit, southpaw fighters tend to be taller by about 2 inches, and on average have over 1.5 inches of reach advantage over orthodox fighters.

Exhibit 7.4: Average Height and Reach by Fighting Stance (in inches)

Stance	Average Height	Average Reach
Orthodox	69.7	72.1
Southpaw	71.7	73.6

To examine if a preferred fighting stance influences fight outcomes, scenarios in which a southpaw fighter faced an orthodox fighter were compared to scenarios in which both fighters had the same stance (both using either orthodox stance or southpaw stance). On average, fighters that are southpaw have a 56% chance of winning a fight against an orthodox opponent. This result suggests that an opponent's southpaw stance places an orthodox fighter at a slight disadvantage, though some of this disadvantage may be an intrinsic result of average height and reach advantages enjoyed by most southpaw fighters, as described above.

CHAPTER EIGHT
PREDICTING FIGHT OUTCOMES

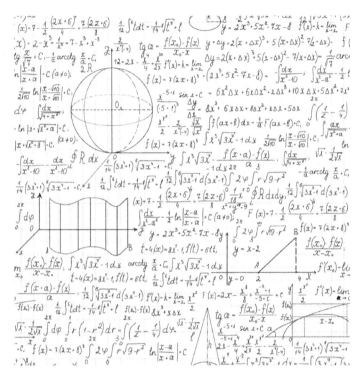

As discussed in the introductory chapter of this book, the desire to understand conditions that foster success in combat has been at the heart of military science for nearly two centuries. Dating back to the 19th century work of Carl von Clausewitz, the dissection of combat conditions into their respective elements has allowed military strategists to identify battlefield approaches that are most likely to result in military success. In his inquiry, Clausewitz examined the battlefield records of thousands of military conflicts, and arrived at objective observations on the optimal path that military commanders can follow when facing their adversaries. For example, Clausewitz discovered that direct confrontations, in which one army marches head-on against an opposing army of equal strength, rarely lead to success. In contrast, engagements in which higher grounds are secured or in which focused effort is deployed on specific sections of the front line lead to greater probabilities of success for the attacking army.

Clausewitz's methodical study of a large number of data points from combat scenarios enriched his work. The results of his analyses were compiled by his wife after his death in the book *On War*, which has been required reading for military strategists around the world since its publication in 1832. In this chapter, we will model our analysis after Clausewitz's approach. Just as Clausewitz was able to utilize the characteristics of each army and conditions of combat to provide predictions for the likelihood of military success, we will examine the combatants' characteristics in an MMA fight context, and use them to develop predictive formulas for success. A range of fighter characteristics discussed throughout this book were used in an extensive statistical analysis involving two hundred MMA fights in order to build a predictive model for determining a fighter's probability of winning a fight.

What Variables Can Be Used for Prediction?

The list of variables to describe fighter characteristics, which were discussed in the previous chapters, will be used to characterize each fighter's standing before a fight. Using a database of completed fights, these characteristics are linked to the eventual outcome of the fight through a statistical modeling technique in order to build a predictive model. The model can then be used for linking fighter characteristics to the probability of winning an upcoming fight. The fighter characteristics that are used in this analysis include the following:

☐ The age difference between the fighter and his opponent

☐ The height difference between the fighter and his opponent

☐ The reach difference between the fighter and his opponent

☐ The fight experience difference between the fighter and his opponent, as measured by the difference in the number of professional MMA fights

☐ Fighter Versatility Index

☐ Fight record ratios related to non-decision wins and losses (discussed in the previous chapter): WKO, WSUB, LKO, LSU

☐ Past win ratio: total number of wins divided by total number of fights

☐ Fighter's stance advantage: The advantage that exists when a southpaw fighter faces an orthodox opponent as discussed in the previous chapter

☐ The fighter's first five professional fight records

☐ Whether or not the fighter is coming off of a recent loss

The central question relates to the ability of the above variables to predict fight outcomes. This is an important question from a range of perspectives because the eventual outcome of fights is often a heavily speculated matter for the media, fans and observers. In addition, matchmakers must ensure that the fights put on a card are likely to have fighters of balanced levels of combat strength so that fights are entertaining. The ability to predict fight outcomes is also relevant to fighters and trainers who need to assess the intensity of the circumstances surrounding an upcoming fight and adjust training and fight preparations accordingly.

If the above variables — many of which are heavily relied upon by speculators — do not have much predictive power, then the value of such speculative conversations related to fight outcomes is minimal. On the other hand, if fight outcomes can be predicted with some accuracy based on the above variables, then there is merit in using these variables to project possible outcomes of fights. It is important to recognize that the list of variables above is motivated by the discussions presented in the earlier chapters as well as the availability of related data. Other variables, such as the characteristics of a fighter's training camp, his state of mind in the days preceding the fight or circumstances related to prefight weight cuts, may also be predictive of fight outcomes but could not be used in this analysis due to lack of access to the data.

What Statistical Method Can Be Used in Order to Predict Fight Outcomes?

The method of analysis used for building this prediction model is binary logistic regression. Logistic regression allows one to use a set of predictor variables (also referred to as "independent variables") such as fighters' height, age and reach, in order to predict the fight outcome ("dependent variable"). The process requires one to provide the logistic regression software with past fight data, in each case profiling all the independent variables (those listed in the section above) and the dependent variable (win or loss). Logistic regression then provides a mathematical formula that can be used for predicting future fight outcomes, in the form of an estimate of the probability of a fighter winning an upcoming fight. This method of analysis, in which a binary outcome (for example a win or a loss) is used as the dependent variable to determine the role of a set of predictors, is heavily used in various fields of science.[19] For example, it is used by political scientists to predict voting behavior of individuals, by marketers to predict consumers' purchase decisions, and by transportation engineers to predict drivers' choice of travel routes[20].

The process of using logistic regression in the context of data from MMA fights is a two-step process. We first use data from a set of fights that have already taken place (called the 'estimation sample') to estimate the predictive formula using logistic regression. The second step includes making sure the formula produced by logistic regression is reliable by applying it to another set of fight data (called the 'holdout sample') in order to assess how accurately the formula is able to predict wins and losses for fights with known results. If, in every case,

[19] J.F. Hair, W.C. Black, B.J. Babin, and R. E. Anderson (2010). *Multivariate Data Analysis*. Prentice Hall; chapter 6.
[20] S.P. Washington, M.G. Karlaftis and F.L. Mannering (2010). *Statistical and Econometric Methods for Transportation Data Analysis*. Chapman and Hall.

the model is able to predict the actual fight outcome (win or loss) correctly, we would have a perfect model. Having a predictive model that can accurately predict every outcome is highly improbable. However, it is important to determine how close one can get to this ideal state. Exhibit 8.1 shows the prediction and testing process.

Exhibit 8.1: Predictive Modeling for Fight Outcomes
Using Logistic Regression

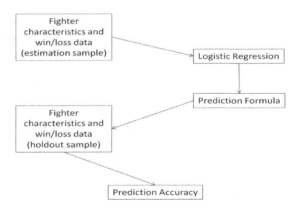

Can Fight Outcomes Be Predicted?

The estimation sample for this analysis consisted of 100 randomly selected MMA fights for which each opponent's characteristics were profiled. The holdout sample consisted of 100 randomly selected fights. Once the logistic regression estimates were obtained from the estimation sample, they were applied to each of the 100 records in the holdout sample to determine the precision by which the model can be used to predict the actual fight outcomes (which are known in the holdout sample), and if the precision of these predictions exceeds statistical baselines. The statistical baseline for a binary outcome is a 50/50 outcome. In other words, since (with the exception of the rare cases of draws and no contests) the outcome of a fight for a given fighter is either a win or a loss, assuming that no more information exists and both fighters are of equal strength, there is a 50% chance for a given fighter to win. From a predictive point of view, the central question then becomes whether we can predict fight outcomes in more than 50% of the cases, and also if there are specific scenarios in which prediction accuracy may be greater.

When estimates obtained from the estimation sample were applied to the holdout sample, the model was able to accurately predict 58% of all fights. While this is an improvement over the baseline of 50% and is statistically significant, it is not a large improvement when practically applied. This finding suggests that the fight characteristics used in this model (many of which are heavily relied upon by observers) do contribute to fight outcomes to some extent. However, other variables not captured in the analysis (for example where a fighter trains, the martial arts styles in which the fighter has trained, the fighter's state of mind before entering the cage, the number of years the fighter has been training, existence of pre-fight injuries) can have a notable effect on fight outcomes as well. These could not be adequately analyzed by the model due to lack of related data.

To determine if some fights can be predicted with greater accuracy, the probability predictions produced by the model were subjected to a cutoff. Predictions that were more definitive in nature – cases in which the model predicted a fighter to have a likelihood of winning greater than 75% or less than 25% – were analyzed. In these cases, the model predicted fight outcomes at a considerably higher level of accuracy. Sixty-eight percent (68%) of such cases were correctly classified by the model. This suggests that, while about half of all fights are difficult to predict with accuracy, the other half – those with very high or very low predicted probabilities of the fighter winning – can be more accurately predicted.

Are the Predictions Useful?

The above analysis demonstrates that the estimates obtained from statistical modeling of fight data can be used to predict fight outcomes. The question of interest is whether the accuracy of these predictions can be of assistance in certain contexts. Sports betting is an industry that has been heavily linked with mixed martial arts. While 68% may be considered a high accuracy of prediction, such predictions are not sufficiently accurate from a sports betting perspective. This is because of the severe penalties that oddsmakers place on predictions that are revealed to be incorrect, and the loss of money waged on a fighter who loses. Predictions produced by this modeling approach are therefore irrelevant and not usable from that perspective.

However, the predictive modeling approach may be quite useful for fighters, trainers, and matchmakers. For fighters, knowing the scientifically predicted odds they face may help motivate intensification of training and improved preparedness for an upcoming fight. It may, therefore, help prioritize a fighter's agenda in advance of a fight. For trainers, knowledge of the odds facing one's fighter may help guide the training program used to enhance the chances of winning. Matchmakers can also utilize such a modeling framework to identify the best matches. When various fighters are being considered for a match, the probability of either fighter winning should ideally be difficult to determine using this model (it should be close to the 50% baseline). In other words, a matchmaker would want to avoid a circumstance in which one fighter is predicted to dominate the fight. For example, a match in which one fighter has a predicted winning probability of 90% would be inappropriate. By avoiding such situations, the resulting fight would most likely be an entertaining and engaging one since the two fighters would present balanced combat capabilities. If the model predicts one fighter to win with a high probability, the combat abilities of the two fighters are then not well-matched, and the fight may be unbalanced. This may lead to significant injuries experienced by the dominated fighter or to the fight ending with an early stoppage by the referee.

CHAPTER 9
FIGHT RITUALS

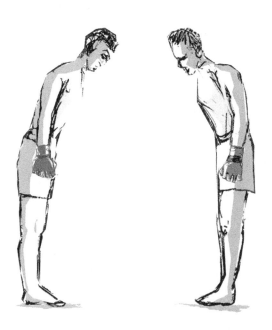

No book on fighting would be complete without some discussion of fighter rituals that precede and follow a fight. In the world of mixed martial arts, fighters exhibit a wide range of rituals. Many fighters exhibit a high degree of spirituality in their pre-fight or post-fight behaviors, for example by tracing the cross across their chest with their hands or pointing to up toward the heavens. In addition, fighters often exhibit behaviors that reflect their states of mind and their perspectives on their opponents. For example, some may choose to bump fists with their opponent upon the start of the fight as a sign of mutual respect, while others may refuse to do so as a reflection of their hostility toward their opponent.

These rituals are a physical manifestation of mental states that each fighter brings into the cage. It would, therefore, be interesting to examine the relationship between rituals and eventual fight outcomes. Rituals are formally defined as a "window on the cultural dynamics by which people make and remake their worlds".[21] Rituals are often invoked when a great degree of uncertainty surrounds an individual or an act, and they can aid the individual by soothing emotional turmoil or providing stability when faced with physical and emotional distress. For this reason, ritualistic practices can be witnessed in a range of competitive sports and are especially prevalent in combat sports.[22]

In this chapter, we will examine the effects of common rituals exhibited by mixed martial arts fighters. These rituals do not directly affect the physical mechanics of combat, but they may have

---

[21] C. Bell (2009). *Ritual Theory, Ritual Practice.* Oxford University Press; p.3.
[22] A. Guttmann (2004). *From Ritual to Record: The Nature of Modern Sports.* Columbia University Press.

indirect effects on events during a fight because of the psychological impact they may have on a fighter. We will examine questions such as whether fighters' acknowledgement of each other at the start of the fight decreases the likelihood of violent endings to the fight (e.g., knockout or submission). We will also examine the relationship between how fights end and the respect and acknowledgment that fighters exhibit toward each other upon fight conclusion.

The data source used for the analyses presented in this chapter is video recordings of 209 mixed martial arts fights, which underwent detailed coding. These recordings were subjected to content-analysis techniques in order to classify the rituals exhibited by each fighter before, during, and after the fight. Content analysis is a well-established research method used in sociology and psychology that translates qualitative data such as exhibition of specific behaviors by an individual or the expression of certain thoughts by a respondent into categories that can be tabulated and subjected to detailed data analysis.[23] The categorized behavioral data resulting from this approach are then correlated with other measures such as fight outcomes and fighter characteristics using statistical techniques.

---

[23] K. Krippendorff (2012), *Content Analysis: An Introduction to its Methodology*. Sage Publications Inc.

107

What Are the Most Common Pre-Fight Acknowledgements Inside the Cage?

After the start of the first round of a fight, immediately before engaging each other in combat, fighters have to make a collaborative decision as to whether or not they will acknowledge each other, for example by bumping fists or tapping gloves. Such a gesture reflects the degree of respect the fighters have toward each other. In situations in which some hostility has preceded the fight (during pre-fight media coverage or the weigh-in, for example), it is customary for the fighters not to exhibit any such gestures of acknowledgment, but to immediately begin combat. Tabulation of these gestures exhibited in the previously mentioned sample was conducted in order to evaluate the types of pre-fight acknowledgements exhibited by fighters, as well as the frequency at which they occur. The results are shown in Exhibit 9.1.

Exhibit 9.1: Typical Pre-Fight Acknowledgments Exhibited by MMA Fighters	
Fist bump	39.9%
No acknowledgment	38.7%
Tapping hands	19.7%
Hand slap	1.4%
Grasping both hands	0.4%

As can be seen from the exhibit, in nearly 4 out of every 10 instances, fighters choose not to acknowledge each other at the start of the fight. Fist bumps, however, account for a similar proportion of prefight acknowledgments. Tapping of hands, which also is reflective of fighters' mutual respect for each other, is exhibited by nearly 2 in every 10 fighters. Overall, more than 60% of fighters exhibit some form of acknowledgement toward their opponent, which is reflective of professionalism that is common in the sport despite its combative and competitive nature.

Does the Fighters' Lack of Mutual Acknowledgement Lead to Violent Endings?

When fighters choose not to acknowledge each other at the beginning of the fight, by not bumping fists, for example, this behavior is often interpreted as an expression of disrespect or hostility between the fighters. The questions of whether or not this expression later manifests as intensity during the events of the fight and if such intensity may result in more violent endings to the fight were studied in this analysis. To determine if such a relationship exists, a cross-tabulation was conducted whereby fighter acknowledgement as a binary variable (acknowledgement or no acknowledgment) was tabulated against the result of a violent ending (knockout, technical knockout, submission) or a decision ending. Exhibit 9.2 shows the relationship.

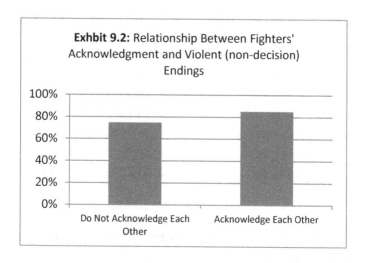

Exhbit 9.2: Relationship Between Fighters' Acknowledgment and Violent (non-decision) Endings

As can be seen from the exhibit, the relationship is the opposite of that which was expected. When fighters do acknowledge each other, there is a greater chance (by 10%) that the fight will end with a knockout, TKO or submission. Fights in which fighters do not acknowledge each other at the beginning of the fight are more likely to have an outcome determined by the judges. The results may indicate that when fighters are less acknowledging of their opponents, they are in a deeper combative state of mind. As a result both their offensive and defensive movements may be more effective, preventing them from being submitted or knocked out by their opponent. Therefore, the outcome of the fight must be decided by the judges as the increased effectiveness of each fighter's approach in the ring eliminates the possibility of an obvious winner. The differences in percentages observed in Exhibit 9.2 were tested using Chi-square analysis and found to be statistically significant (p<.05, χ^2= 4.2; Φ =0.12).

Does Taking the Center of the Cage in the Opening Round Matter?

The center of the cage is a highly strategic position as the fighter in that position can dictate the pace of the fight. It allows the fighter to advance on his opponent and, if needed, to push the opponent toward the walls of the cage, enabling takedowns or close-up strikes. In addition, by taking the center position in the cage, one is able to prevent strikes by moving backwards. This position also enables takedown defense as there is more space to execute defensive grappling techniques. In addition to these tactical benefits, a fighter's decision to take the center of the cage may be expressive of a more aggressive state of mind. Therefore, an emerging question relates to the fight outcomes for fighters who choose to take the center of the cage upon the start of the fight. To explore this question, fighters' physical position at the start of the first round was coded (which fighter takes the center of the cage first) and analyzed with respect to the eventual outcome of the fight. The results show no statistically significant difference in fight outcome as a result of the starting position of the fighter, with equal likelihood of winning the fight despite the fighter's position in the first few seconds of the opening round.

Do Fighters Typically Carry Over Lack of Mutual Acknowledgement to the End of the Fight?

An interesting question with regards to fighters' approach to acknowledging each other relates to how they choose to behave at the end of the fight. At the end of the fight, either at the end of the last round or when the fight result is announced, fighters who remain standing may choose to acknowledge each other, for example by shaking hands or bowing to each other. They may also choose not to express any gestures of acknowledgment. To gain a better understanding of fighters' end-of-fight acknowledgment behaviors, video recordings of fight endings were subjected to content analysis procedures, and acknowledgment gestures were categorized and tabulated.

The question of interest is whether the fighters' acknowledgement of the opponent carries over from the start of the fight to the end of the fight. For example, if a fighter had chosen not to acknowledge his opponent at the start of the fight, and continues not to acknowledge his opponent at the end of the fight, the behavior reflects a sense of consistency in fighter mentality. To explore the degree of consistency in acknowledgment behavior, fighters' pre-fight and post-fight acknowledgement behaviors were cross-tabulated. The results are shown in Exhibit 9.3. The Y-axis in this exhibit represents the probability of acknowledging the opponent at the end of the fight.

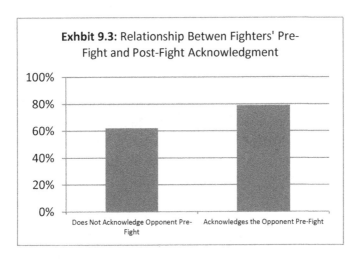

Exhbit 9.3: Relationship Betwen Fighters' Pre-Fight and Post-Fight Acknowledgment

As can be seen in the exhibit, a fighter who chooses not to acknowledge his opponent at the start of the fight is less likely to acknowledge his opponent at the end of the fight. On the other hand, in nearly 80% of cases where fighters acknowledge each other at the start of the fight, they demonstrate the same behavior at the end of the fight. This pattern of behavior exhibits consistency in the acknowledgement decisions of fighters and may be reflective of a deeper sense of respect or hostility toward the opponent that persists even after the completion of the fight. The differences in percentages observed were tested using Chi-square analysis and found to be statistically significant (p<.01, χ^2= 7.3; Φ =0.18).

How Frequently Do Winners Exhibit Signs of Spirituality at the End of the Fight?

At the end of the fight, some winning fighters exhibit signs of spirituality. These signs may include tracing the cross on one's chest, pointing to the heavens, or kneeling down to the earth, as well as other gestures often associated with religious symbolism. These end-of-fight rituals were tabulated for winning fighters in order to determine the frequency at which they occur. Overall, spiritual gestures were exhibited by 17% of the winning fighters at the end of the fight. It is important to note that this figure is most likely underestimating the actual exhibition of spirituality, as such gestures may have not been captured in the video footage coded in this study. In addition, such gestures may take place in more private settings rather than in front of cage side cameras. Statistical analysis showed that the display of spirituality is unaffected by the fighters' nationality and age. Nevertheless, the fact that many winning fighters choose to express their spirituality openly demonstrates the profound psychological and emotional forces involved in preparing an individual to enter the cage and leaving as the victor.

CHAPTER TEN
IMPLICATIONS FOR THE FUTURE OF MIXED MARTIAL ARTS

In this chapter, we will discuss the implications of the key findings from earlier chapters. We will examine the implications from three different perspectives: from the perspective of fight promoters and regulators; how the results may influence the role of medical care providers in sanctioned MMA fights; how fighters and trainers may modify their fight preparations based on the findings in this book.

Implications for Fight Promoters and Regulators

(1) Careful Consideration Needs to Be Given to Combatants' Relative Ages. The results in Chapter 3 indicate that significant variations in fighter ability (as measured by likelihood of winning fights) exist as a result of differences in combatants' ages (e.g., Exhibits 3.2 and 3.5). Younger fighters have a higher rate of success than older fighters. Matching younger fighters against older fighters may create predictable fight results favoring younger fighters. For this reason, fight promoters must pay closer attention to the relative ages of the fighters being matched in order to create fair and balanced fights and to generate more entertaining events.

(2) Improving Fighter Safety: The results shown in Chapter 4 indicate that average fighter injury counts have declined over the years (e.g., Exhibit 4.2). The declining rate of injuries can be attributed to improved defensive training; it can also be attributed to a more proactive stance taken by the referees, which limits injuries to the fighters. The decline in fighter injuries over time not only increases the safety of the sport for the

fighters, but also makes it a more enjoyable and marketable form of entertainment for the public.

(3) Matchmaking in order to Ensure Diversity in Fight Styles of Combatants: The results of Chapter 5 show that the number of fights that conclude with decisions are on the rise (e.g., Exhibit 5.4). Though fights that end with decisions can elongate tournaments, they are also perceived as less entertaining by spectators. To increase the entertainment value of MMA events, matchmakers need to create fight contexts that bring together fighters of differing backgrounds and styles. This improves the likelihood of fights ending with non-decision outcomes and increases the entertainment value of the card.

(4) Utilizing Standardized Versatility Measures in Matchmaking: The results in chapters 6 and 7 demonstrate that fighter ability can be quantified in standardized form, such as the Fighter Versatility Index, and associated win/loss ratios. These figures, alongside predictive modeling (an example of which was shown in Chapter 8) can be used to ensure that fighters who are matched against each other are equally capable. Matching a dominant fighter against an inferior fighter not only creates an unbalanced circumstance, but it may also result in significant injuries to the dominated fighter and lead to an uninteresting and one-sided event. Use of predictive modeling to match fighters of equal strength can create fight

cards that are more entertaining to the spectators and challenging for the fighters. The various win and loss ratios can also be used to further guide matchmaking decisions.

(5) Recognizing Early Indicators of Fighter Superiority: One of the common patterns in the win/loss history of superior fighters in mixed martial arts is the highly predictive quality of win outcomes for the first 5 professional MMA fights. As was shown in Exhibit 6.7, fighters who won their first few professional fights tend to progress further in the profession than most of the fighters who had losses during the early stages of their professional careers. Many of the fighters from the first group eventually take on contender or championship positions.

(6) Consideration Given to Frame Size Rather than Weight: In the early days of mixed martial arts, many organizations did not have weight classes. Fighters of all sizes were able to face each other. As the sport grew and more spectators were attracted to the sport, concerns also grew about unbalanced fight scenarios in which heavier fighters were matched against smaller opponents because lighter fighters tended to be dominated by their opponents. This resulted in the enforcement of weight classes. However, questions remain as to the appropriateness of weight class as a categorization and matching

mechanism for fighters. The results of Chapter 7 indicate that a fighter's reach advantage over his opponent can significantly improve his chances of winning a fight (Exhibit 7.1). Similarly, a height advantage produces favorable results (Exhibit 7.3). For these reasons, it is of considerable advantage to fighters of larger frame to lose significant amounts of weight before fights in order to qualify for considerably lower weight classes and, as a result, to be matched with fighters of much smaller frames. This not only puts the smaller fighter at a disadvantage, but also puts at risk the health of the larger fighter who has lost a significant amount of weight, often through dehydration procedures. Regulators and fight promoters may, therefore, need to consider the possibility of establishing a fighter classification system based on the fighters' frames rather than weight.

Implications for Medical Care Providers:

(1) Addressing the Medical Needs of Fighters Above the Age of 30: The results of this study indicate that older fighters are at significantly greater risk of experiencing injuries during an MMA fight (e.g., Exhibit 4.3). In addition, when a fighter is matched against a younger fighter, his chances of being injured increase by nearly 50% (Exhibit 4.4). For this reason, medical care providers in MMA events must be more vigilant when the matched opponents have disparate ages. In cases where

119

emergency medical care and evacuation to an emergency medical facility are needed, the heightened state of alertness may help in the prioritization of medical resources to address the potential medical needs of older fighters. Advanced preparations and precautions taken by emergency medical staff who are alerted to this information may facilitate on-site care or transport to emergency medical centers as needed in order to provide optimal treatment for injuries sustained by older MMA fighters

(2) *Planning for Special Needs During Heavy Weight Fights:* The results of this study show that a fighter's weight class does not influence the number of injuries received. However, weight class has a direct impact on the method by which non-decision fight conclusions are arrived at (e.g., Exhibit 3.7). Fights in the heavier weight classes are more likely to conclude with a KO or TKO, and fights in the lighter weight classes are more likely to conclude with submissions. As a result, on-site medical care providers can anticipate injuries resulting from strikes (e.g., concussions, facial laceration) more frequently for fights in higher weight classes. Given the severe nature of these injuries, it is essential to plan for the required medical resources in advance fights in higher weight classes.

Implications for Trainers and Fighters:

(1) Special Preparations Needed for Facing Younger Opponents: The results of Chapter 3 show that there is a clear winning advantage for younger fighters when facing older opponents (e.g., Exhibit 3.5). When preparing for a fight, it is important to recognize that the opponent's age may influence the fighter's probability of winning a fight. It is essential that both fighter and trainer take additional measures to adjust fight preparations and training to increase the likelihood of success when matched against a younger fighter.

(2) Recognizing the Evolution of Fighting Methods in Preparing Fighters of Different Ages: The results of Chapter 3 also demonstrate that fighters' skills and fighting styles evolve as they age (e.g., Exhibit 3.4). Younger fighters typically win through submissions while older fighters typically win through KO or TKO. This shift may result in part from differences in fighter training. Younger fighters have become more familiar with submission fighting methods, and older fighters are more accustomed to traditional combat styles such as boxing, Muay Thai, Karate and kickboxing. Fight preparations, therefore, must take such differences into account. Trainers may also benefit from diversifying the skill sets of their fighters. This may be especially helpful when training younger fighters who may not be as accustomed to striking as are their older opponents. Similarly, trainers

need to emphasize the development of submission fighting skills for their older fighters.

(3) Mentally Preparing Fighters for the Unique Challenges of Specific Fight Contexts: The results of Chapter 5 demonstrate significant effects of fight context on performance. For example, the location of a fight can influence the underlying probability of a win. Hometown fighters have a slight advantage over their out-of-town opponents (e.g., Exhibit 5.6). Furthermore, the results suggest that the method by which a fighter achieves a non-decision end to a fight evolves through the fight rounds (e.g., Exhibit 5.2) and that title fights are more likely to be concluded by KO and TKO than non-title fights (e.g., Exhibit 5.1). The results of Chapter 6 also demonstrate that a fighter's recent fight history affects his probability of winning. As shown in Exhibit 6.7, a fighter that is coming off of a loss has a much stronger drive to win the next fight and, therefore, win rates for such fighters can be higher by approximately 10% when compared to win rates for fighters who are coming off of a win. Therefore, when facing an opponent who is coming off of a loss, one needs to be alert to the opponent's increased level of motivation and the possibility that it may result in more challenging scenarios inside the cage. These contextual factors can significantly affect the mental state of fighters, and trainers must, therefore, pay careful attention when preparing

their fighters for specific fight contexts discussed in this book.

(4) Utilizing Fighter Versatility Measures in Preparing for Fights: The Fighter Versatility Index and the associated win/loss ratios discussed in Chapter 6 summarize a fighter's abilities in the form of numeric measures that can be compared across fighters. These measures can identify areas in which a fighter exhibits strength as well as areas in which he may be vulnerable. They may also be predictive in determining fight outcomes, as demonstrated in the predictive modeling discussions of Chapter 8. Trainers must, therefore, pay close attention to these measures in order to quantify the capabilities of their fighters as well as those of their opponents, and to orient training programs to minimize shortcomings of one's own fighter while capitalizing on the weaknesses of the opponent.

(5) Beware of Frame Size Differences: The analyses presented in Chapter 7 demonstrated the profound impact that a fighter's frame as measured by reach and height can have on his likelihood of winning fights (for example, as shown in Exhibits 7.1 and 7.3). For this reason, fighters should pay close attention to any advantages or disadvantages they may have in terms of reach or height. When facing fighters of larger frame, pre-fight preparations and training should focus on tactics and maneuvers that overcome and

neutralize the opponent's reach or height advantage.

(6) Special Preparations When Facing Southpaw Fighters: The analyses presented in Chapter 7 demonstrate that 3 out of every 4 fighters have an orthodox stance and the remaining 25% of fighters are southpaw. This often places southpaw fighters at an advantage since their opponents may not have had frequent opportunities to spar and train with southpaw opponents. Fighting in a southpaw stance, especially when enjoying a reach advantage, provides the fighter with opportunities for specific strikes (e.g., left high kick, right hook punch) with which orthodox fighters may not have had sufficient experience to develop a defense. For this reason, orthodox fighters facing a southpaw opponent need to ensure that they practice sufficiently and train with southpaw sparring partners in advance of the fight. It can also be argued that a change in the training discipline of MMA fighters should be put in place by trainers in order to return to the roots of striking traditions of Kung Fu and Karate in which fighters are trained to fight both in orthodox and southpaw stances. Such a shift would eliminate disadvantages currently facing orthodox fighters.

Concluding Thoughts

While mixed martial arts has grown in popularity and has matured into a mainstream sport over the past two decades, the potential for evolution and growth still exists. One of the biggest areas for potential growth is women's MMA. Due to data limitations, this book focuses exclusively on men's MMA; however, as the popularity of women's MMA grows, examination of topics studied in this book will be necessary in the context of data from women's MMA.

As it has been in the past, the future of MMA will be influenced by the evolution of regulations governing the sport. In the early years of MMA, for example, fighters were allowed to wear full body uniforms such as the gi. Wearing such clothing created more realistic situations for the fighters, representative of hand-to-hand street fights. Requiring fighters to wear full body uniforms can drastically change the sport by increasing the ease of executing certain moves, such as throws and submissions; therefore, new forms of offense and defense could be introduced. Furthermore, in the early days of MMA, a more diverse range of strikes were allowed. A return to some of these traditions may in fact make MMA more applicable as a practical self-defense technique and increase its external validity outside the regulated confines of the cage.

It is also important to recognize that while statistical analysis was used in this book, there are limits in terms of the degree by which the findings can be generalized. For example, one of the greatest concerns remains to be the safety of the fighters and the severity of injuries experienced. Between 2007 and 2014, four fighters lost their lives as a result of injuries experienced during sanctioned bouts. Through the years, another six fighters have lost their lives in unsanctioned events. Of the total of 10 deaths in MMA competition, seven have occurred within the past decade, and six have been cases of fighters aged 30 or higher. It is therefore important for regulators and health care professionals to clearly understand the circumstances that resulted in these deaths, and to take the necessary steps to prevent future loss of life.

In addition to the implications listed earlier in this chapter, this book demonstrates the power of statistical analysis when applied to mixed martial arts fight records in order to identify contributors to fighting success and to improve fighter safety. It is, therefore, hoped that the results of this work will inform the many professionals committed to this fascinating and evolving sport, and encourage innovative thinking to advance mixed martial arts.

AUTHOR'S BIOGRAPHY

Hooman Estelami is a professor of marketing at the Graduate School of Business, Fordham University. He received his Ph.D. from Columbia University and his MBA from McGill University. His areas of research specialization are pricing, financial services marketing, customer service management, and distance education. He is the author of three books: (*Marketing Financial Services; Marketing Turnarounds; Frontiers of Distance Learning in Business Education*). He is the former associate editor of the *Journal of Product and Brand Management,* a current editor of the *International Journal of Bank Marketing,* and has been studying martial arts for nearly three decades. He can be reached at estelami@fordham.edu.

Made in the USA
Middletown, DE
05 March 2019